CAMBRIDGE LIBRARY COLLECTION

Books of enduring scholarly value

Archaeology

The discovery of material remains from the recent or the ancient past has always been a source of fascination, but the development of archaeology as an academic discipline which interpreted such finds is relatively recent. It was the work of Winckelmann at Pompeii in the 1760s which first revealed the potential of systematic excavation to scholars and the wider public. Pioneering figures of the nineteenth century such as Schliemann, Layard and Petrie transformed archaeology from a search for ancient artifacts, by means as crude as using gunpowder to break into a tomb, to a science which drew from a wide range of disciplines - ancient languages and literature, geology, chemistry, social history - to increase our understanding of human life and society in the remote past.

A Commentary on the Cuneiform Inscriptions of Babylonia and Assyria

This publication released to a wider audience the work on Assyrian inscriptions of Sir Henry Rawlinson (1810–95), who had begun his career in the East India Company in Persia and Afghanistan, where his exceptional linguistic skills were recognised. He had been studying the monumental, trilingual (in Old Persian, Elamite and Babylonian) Behistun inscription of Darius the Great since 1836, and, building on the earlier research of Georg Friedrich Grotefend, delivered a summary of his progress in decipherment to the Royal Asiatic Society early in 1850. He intended to follow it up with a longer book, but was anxious to gain credit for primacy (which was questioned at the time and still remains controversial), and so published this short work in March 1850. It states Rawlinson's theories, and offers a linguistic and archaeological background to his work, along with his interpretation of king lists and other inscriptions.

Cambridge University Press has long been a pioneer in the reissuing of out-of-print titles from its own backlist, producing digital reprints of books that are still sought after by scholars and students but could not be reprinted economically using traditional technology. The Cambridge Library Collection extends this activity to a wider range of books which are still of importance to researchers and professionals, either for the source material they contain, or as landmarks in the history of their academic discipline.

Drawing from the world-renowned collections in the Cambridge University Library and other partner libraries, and guided by the advice of experts in each subject area, Cambridge University Press is using state-of-the-art scanning machines in its own Printing House to capture the content of each book selected for inclusion. The files are processed to give a consistently clear, crisp image, and the books finished to the high quality standard for which the Press is recognised around the world. The latest print-on-demand technology ensures that the books will remain available indefinitely, and that orders for single or multiple copies can quickly be supplied.

The Cambridge Library Collection brings back to life books of enduring scholarly value (including out-of-copyright works originally issued by other publishers) across a wide range of disciplines in the humanities and social sciences and in science and technology.

A Commentary on the Cuneiform Inscriptions of Babylonia and Assyria

*Including Readings of the Inscription
on the Nimrud Obelisk,
and a Brief Notice of the Ancient Kings
of Nineveh and Babylon*

Henry Creswicke Rawlinson

CAMBRIDGE
UNIVERSITY PRESS

CAMBRIDGE
UNIVERSITY PRESS

University Printing House, Cambridge, CB2 8BS, United Kingdom

Cambridge University Press is part of the University of Cambridge.

It furthers the University's mission by disseminating knowledge in the pursuit of
education, learning and research at the highest international levels of excellence.

www.cambridge.org
Information on this title: www.cambridge.org/9781108077477

This edition first published 1850
This digitally printed version 2014

ISBN 978-1-108-07747-7 Paperback

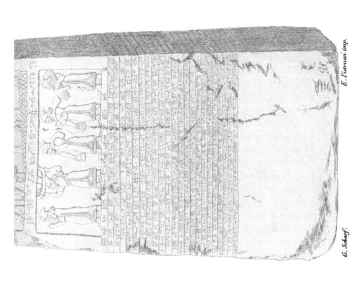

G. Scharf.

E. Vincent imp.

The Nimrud Obelisk in the British Museum.

A COMMENTARY

ON THE

CUNEIFORM INSCRIPTIONS

OF

BABYLONIA AND ASSYRIA;

INCLUDING READINGS OF THE

INSCRIPTION ON THE NIMRUD OBELISK,

AND A BRIEF NOTICE OF

THE ANCIENT KINGS OF NINEVEH AND BABYLON.

———

READ BEFORE THE ROYAL ASIATIC SOCIETY;

BY

MAJOR H. C. RAWLINSON.

QUOT RAMI TOT ARBORES.

LONDON:

JOHN W. PARKER, WEST STRAND.

———

1850.

LONDON
PRINTED BY HARRISON AND SON,
ST. MARTIN'S LANE.

INSCRIPTIONS OF ASSYRIA AND BABYLONIA.

PRELIMINARY NOTICE.

When I drew up the following Notes upon the Inscriptions of Babylonia and Assyria, and read them at the Royal Asiatic Society's Meetings of January 19th, and February 16th, I had no intention of publishing them in their present form. I merely wished, as much interest had been excited by the exhibition of the Nineveh marbles, to satisfy public curiosity, by presenting at once, and in a popular shape, a general view of the results at which I had arrived in my labours on the Inscriptions ; and I judged that this object would be more conveniently attained by oral communication than by publication in the pages of a Scientific Journal. At the same time, of course, I proposed to follow up the oral communication, by publishing with the least practicable delay, a full exposition of the machinery which I had employed both for deciphering and rendering intelligible the Inscriptions, and during the interval which would thus elapse between announcement and proof, I trusted that, if inquiry were not altogether suspended, philologers and palæographers would, at any rate, refrain from pronouncing upon the validity of my system of interpretation.

It has since, however, been suggested to me, that much inconvenience may arise from this partition of the subject. Weeks, perhaps months, will be required to carry through the press the Memoir in its complete state, and with all its typographical illustrations; and if, accordingly, upon the date of the appearance of the Memoir in print were made to depend the originality of the matter contained in it, my claim to a priority of, or even to independent, discovery might be very seriously endangered ; for many inquirers are known to be already in the field, and the clue afforded to the rectification of phonetic values by the numerous readings which I have given in my Lectures of proper names, both historical and geographical, might thus lead to

B

the announcement in other quarters of the same results, in antici-
pation of the publication of my own translations. Without wishing
then to impute any spirit of unfairness to the parties with whom I am
competing, with every disposition indeed to unite cordially with them
in disentangling the very intricate questions upon which we are
engaged, I now think it advisable, for the due authentication of my
own researches, to place on record the various discoveries, philological, historical, and geographical, in connection with the Inscriptions
of Assyria and Babylonia, which I announced to the Royal Asiatic
Society upon January 19th, and February 16th of the present year;
and I venture accordingly, notwithstanding their popular character,
to print the Lectures delivered on those occasions; merely transposing
the arrangement of the materials so as to form a continuous sketch,
and appending, in a series of notes, such illustrations as appear indis-
pensable to a proper intelligence of the subject.

H. C. R.

March 1, 1850.

---

*Notes on the Inscriptions of Assyria and Babylonia; read at the
Royal Asiatic Society's Meetings of* 19th *January and* 16th *February,* 1850.

BEFORE undertaking the investigation of the obscure subject of
Assyrian history, I propose to explain briefly the means by which the
Inscriptions of Nineveh and Babylon have been rendered legible, and
to take a cursory view of the nature and structure of the alphabet
employed in them. It will also, I think, be desirable to notice such
characteristics of grammar and of speech, as shall be sufficient to
satisfy philologers, that there are ample grounds for classing the ancient vernacular dialects of the Tigris and the Euphrates with that
family of languages that we are accustomed to term Semitic, and which
will perhaps further show, that the connection of the Assyrian and
Babylonian is almost as close with the African, as with the Asiatic
branch of the so-called Semitic family.

I commence with an explanation of the process of decipherment.
There are found in many parts of Persia, either graven on the native
rock, as at Hamadan, at Van, and Behistun, or sculptured on the

walls of the ancient palaces, as at Persepolis and Pasargadæ, Cuneiform Inscriptions which record the glories of the House of Achæ-
menes. These Inscriptions are, in almost every instance, trilingual
and triliteral. They are engraved in three different languages, and
each language has its peculiar alphabet; the alphabets, indeed, varying
from each other, not merely in the characters being formed by a different assortment of the elemental signs which we are accustomed to
term the arrow-head and wedge, but in their whole phonetic structure
and organization. The object, of course, of engraving the records in
three different languages was to render them generally intelligible.
Precisely, indeed, as at the present day, a Governor of Baghdad, who
wished to publish an edict for general information, would be obliged
to employ three languages, the Persian, Turkish, and Arabic; so in
the time of Cyrus and Darius, when the ethnographical constitution of
the empire was subject to the same general division, was it necessary to address the population in the three different languages from
which have sprung the modern Persian, Turkish, and Arabic, or at
any rate in the three languages which represented at the time those
three great lingual families. To this fashion, then, or necessity of
triple publication, are we indebted for our knowledge of the Assyrian
Inscriptions. I need not describe the steps by which the Persian
Cuneiform Alphabet was first deciphered and the language was subsequently brought to light, for full details have been already published in the Society's Journal; but I may notice as an illustration of
the great success which has attended the efforts of myself and other
students in this preliminary branch of the inquiry, that there are probably not more than twenty words in the whole range of the Persian
Cuneiform records, upon the meaning, grammatical condition, or
etymology of which, any doubt or difference of opinion can be said at
present to exist.

As the Greek translation, then, on the Rosetta Stone first led the
way to the decipherment of the hieroglyphic writing of Egypt, so
have the Persian texts of the trilingual Cuneiform tablets served as a
stepping-stone to the intelligence of the Assyrian and Babylonian
Inscriptions. The tablets of Behistun, of Nakhsh-i-Rustam, and Persepolis, have in the first place furnished a list of more than eighty
proper names, of which the true pronunciation is fixed by their Persian
orthography, and of which we have also the Babylonian equivalents.
A careful comparison of these duplicate forms of writing the same
name, and a due appreciation of the phonetic distinctions peculiar to
the two languages, have then supplied the means of determining with
more or less of certainty, the value of about one hundred Babylonian

characters, and a very excellent basis has been thus determined for a complete arrangement of the Alphabet. The next step has been to collate Inscriptions, and to ascertain or infer from the variant orthographies of the same name, (and particularly the same geographical name) the homophones of each known alphabetical power. In this stage of the inquiry much caution, or, if I may so call it, "*critique,*" has been rendered necessary; for although two Inscriptions may be absolutely identical in sense, and even in expression, it does not by any means follow that wherever one text may differ from the other, we are justified in supposing that we have found alphabetical variants. Many sources of variety exist, besides the employment of homophones. Ideographs or abbreviations may be substituted for words expressed phonetically; sometimes the allocation is altered; sometimes synonyms are made use of; grammatical suffixes and affixes again may be employed or suppressed, or modified at option. It requires, in fact, a most ample field of comparison, a certain familiarity with the language, and, above all, much experience in the dialectic changes, and in the varieties of alphabetical expression, before variant characters can be determined with any certainty. By mere comparison, however, repeated in a multitude of instances, so as to reduce almost infinitely the chance of error, I have added nearly fifty characters to the hundred which were previously known through the Persian key; and to this acquaintance with the phonetic value of about one hundred and fifty signs, is, I believe, limited my present knowledge of the Babylonian and Assyrian alphabets.

I will now offer a few remarks on the nature and structure of these alphabets. That the employment of the Cuneiform character originated in Assyria, while the system of writing to which it was adapted was borrowed from Egypt, will hardly admit of question. Whether the Cuneiform letters, in their primitive shapes, were intended like the hieroglyphs to represent actual objects, and were afterwards degraded to their present forms; or whether the point of departure was from the Hieratic, or perhaps the Demotic character, the first change from a picture to a sign having thus taken place before Assyria formed her alphabet, I will not undertake to decide; but the whole structure of the Assyrian graphic system evidently betrays an Egyptian origin. The alphabet is partly ideographic and partly phonetic, and the phonetic signs are in some cases syllabic, and in others literal. Where a sign represents a syllable, I conjecture that the syllable in question may have been the specific name of the object which the sign was supposed to depict; whilst in cases where a single alphabetical power appertains to the sign, it would seem as if that power had been the dominant sound in the name of the object. In this way, at any rate, are we alone, I think, able to account for the anomalous condition of many of the Assyrian signs, which sometimes represent phonetically a complete syllable, and sometimes one only of the sounds of which the syllable is composed[1]. It cannot certainly be maintained that the phonetic portion of the alphabet is altogether syllabic, or, that every phonetic sign represents a complete and uniform articulation. There is, it may be admitted, an extensive syllabarium, but at the same time many of the characters can only be explained as single consonants. These characters again may be usually distinguished as initial and terminal; that is, the vowel sound which is their necessary accompaniment, and which must be supplied according to the requirements of the language, precedes one class of signs and follows another, but in a few instances the character may be employed either to open or close an articulation indifferently; and the entire phonetic structure is thus shown to be in so rude and elementary a state, as to defy the attempt to reduce it to any definite system. A still more formidable difficulty, one, indeed, of which I can only remotely conjecture the explanation, is, that certain characters represent two entirely dissimilar sounds,—sounds so dissimilar, that neither can they be brought into relation with each other, nor, even supposing the sign properly to denote a syllable, which syllable on occasion may be compressed into its dominant sound, will the other power be found to enter at all into the full and original articulation[2].

---

[1] There are thus a series of characters which fluctuate between *t* and *b*, such as 𒁹, ⟩⟨, ⟩⟨, &c. They represent sometimes the complete syllable, but more usually one only of the component sounds. They may perhaps be illustrated by a comparison with the Sanskrit द्विः, which has produced δίς in Greek, and *bis* in Latin. Many other characters also have double powers; the 𒂍 represents indifferently the *r* and *s*, and at Behistun the 𒁹 for *t*, is undistinguishable from the sign which answers to *Par*.

[2] I take for an example the character 𒀸. This sign certainly represents phonetically an *aleph*, 𐤀, but it is also the ideograph for "a son," and in that capacity must, I think, be sounded *bar*. The same sound of *bar* would seem to appertain to it in the name of the Euphrates, where as the initial sign it replaces 𒌋 *b*, or 𒁇 *bar*, but as the final letter of the name of Nineveh (𒌷𒉌 or 𒌷𒉌) it must be a simple labial; while in the names of Nabopolasser, (the father of Nebuchadnezzar) and Sardanapalus, we must give to the sign in question the pronunciation of *pal*, that articulation, pro-

Some of these anomalies belong to the graphic system of Egypt, but some appear peculiar to Assyria. In many other respects, however, the identity of the two systems is complete. Non-phonetic signs are used as determinatives, precisely in the same manner, though not perhaps to the same extent, as in Egyptian, and the names of the gods are represented by signs, which appear in some cases to be arbitrary monograms, but which are more generally, either the dominant sound of the name, or its initial phonetic power [1], which is used for the same purpose in the Demotic alphabet of Egypt. There is also to be remarked the same poverty of the elemental alphabetical sounds; the same want of distinction between the hard and soft pronunciation of the consonants; the same mutation of the liquids and other phonetic powers not strictly homogeneous [2]; the same extensive employment of homophones. The whole system, indeed, of homophones is essentially Egyptian, and could only, I think, have arisen with a nation which made use of picture writing before it attempted alphabetical expression.

In some respects the Assyrian alphabet is even more difficult to be made out than the Egyptian. In the latter, the object depicted can almost always be recognized, and the Coptic name of the object will usually give, in its initial sound, the phonetic power of the hieroglyph; whereas in Assyrian, the machinery by which the power is evolved is altogether obscure—we neither know the object represented, nor if we did know it, should we be able to ascertain its Assyrian name—

bably being considered by the Assyrians and Babylonians to be phonetically identical with *bar*.

[1] For instance, the ordinary sign for Bel is a simple B, ►𝌆; ⎮ *s* stands for *Sut;* ⧻ for *Husi*. In many cases, however, the monograms seem to be arbitrary, as in ⊨ for *Nit;* ✳, ⧻⊢ or ►⬚ for *Nebo;* ⟨ for *Hem;* ⟪⟪ another sign for *Bel;* ⊨⧻ for *Sut,* &c., &c. The phonetic rendering of proper names in Assyrian depends almost entirely on a full understanding of the Pantheon, and this is unfortunately the most difficult branch perhaps of the whole Cuneiform inquiry.

[2] I refer to the interchange of the *l* and *v*, exemplified in such characters as ⟨⊢⎮, ⟨⊢⎮⎮, ⟪⊨⎮⸴⎮, and also in ⊨⎮⊢⎮⎮ or ⊨⎮⊞, ⟨⎮⬚⎮ or ⟨⎮⬚⧻. Many other signs represent the *l,* and *d,* or *t,* indifferently, such as ►⊨⎮ or ✕⎮, ⧻⎮⎮ or ⧻⊨⎮⎮, &c. There is also the greatest possible difficulty in distinguishing between the *k,* and the *d,* or *t;* and the gutturals and sibilants everywhere interchange.

everything has to be subjected to the "experimentum crucis;" and although, in working out this tentative process, the reduced number of the Assyrian signs, the key of eighty proper names, and the unlimited facilities for comparison, tend essentially to lessen the labour, it may be doubted if these united aids are equivalent to the single advantage which Egyptologers enjoy of being able to apply the Coptic vocabulary to the elimination of the phonetic powers of the hieroglyphic signs.

With regard also to the employment of the Cuneiform characters, it is important to observe, that the Assyrian alphabet, with its many imperfections, its most inconvenient laxity, and its cumbrous array of homophones, continued, from the time when it was first organized upon an Egyptian model, up to the period, probably, of the reign of Cyrus the Great, to be the one sole type of writing employed by all the nations of Western Asia, from Syria to the heart of Persia: and, what is still more remarkable, the Assyrian alphabet was thus adopted without reference to the language, or even to the class of language, to which it was required to be applied. There is, thus, no doubt but that the alphabets of Assyria, of Armenia, of Babylonia, of Susiana, and of Elymais are, so far as essentials are concerned, one and the same; there are peculiarities of form, a limitation of usage, an affection for certain favourite characters, incidental to each of the localities; but unquestionably the alphabets are "au fond" identical, while the language of Armenia certainly, and the languages of Susiana and Elymais probably, are not of the same stock even as the dialects spoken in Assyria and Babylonia.

Having shown the means by which a knowledge has been obtained of the Assyrian alphabet, I now proceed to consider the language. The same process which led to the identification of the signs of the alphabet was afterwards applied to the language; that is, as duplicate names determined the value of the Assyrian characters, so did duplicate phrases give the meaning of the Babylonian vocables, and afford an insight into the grammatical structure of the tongue. The stately but sterile formula of Royal commemoration, to which are devoted all the ordinary trilingual tablets of Persia, were certainly anything but favourable to this reanimation of a lost language; but still they were not without their use. They furnished a basis of interpretation, which was afterwards improved and enlarged by a careful dissection of the Inscription which is found on the tomb of Darius at Nakhsh-i-Rustam[1], and by a minute analysis of the fragments which remain

---

[1] I take this opportunity of mentioning that I am indebted to the late Mr. Tasker for a very excellent copy of the Nakhsh-i-Rustam Babylonian Inscrip-

of the great Babylonian translation at Behistun. If the Behistun Inscription had been recovered in as perfect a state as the less celebrated record at Nakhsh-i-Rustam, all the essential difficulties of decipherment would have been at once overcome. There is so much variety, both of matter and of idiom, in the former document, that a complete and rigid translation of the Persian text in the Babylonian character and language would have furnished materials for a grammar and compendious vocabulary. Unfortunately, however, the left half, or perhaps a larger portion even, of the tablet is entirely destroyed, and we have thus the mere endings of the lines throughout the entire length of the Inscription; the fragments which in several of the most interesting passages are alone legible, being not only insufficient to resolve difficulties, but sometimes actually affording of themselves fresh enigmas for solution.

I will frankly confess, indeed, that after having mastered every Babylonian letter, and every Babylonian word, to which any clue existed in the trilingual tablets, either by direct evidence or by induction, I have been tempted, on more occasions than one, in striving to apply the key thus obtained to the interpretation of the Assyrian Inscriptions, to abandon the study altogether in utter despair of arriving at any satisfactory result. It would be affectation to pretend that, because I can ascertain the general purport of an inscription, or, because I can read and approximately render a plain historical record like that upon the Nineveh Obelisk, I am really a complete master of the ancient Assyrian language. It would be disingenuous to slur over the broad fact, that the science of Assyrian decipherment is yet in its infancy. Let it be remembered, that although fifty years have elapsed since the Rosetta Stone was first discovered, and its value was recognized as a partial key to the hieroglyphs, during which period many of the most powerful intellects of modern Europe have devoted themselves to the study of Egyptian; nevertheless, that study, as a distinct branch of philology, has hardly yet passed through its first preliminary stage of cultivation. How, then, can it be expected, that in studying Assyrian, with an alphabet scarcely less difficult, and with a language far more difficult than the Egyptian,—with no Plutarch to dissect the Pantheon and supply the names of the gods,—no Manetho or Eratosthenes to

tion, a copy, indeed, so good, that, with the exception of a few letters, I have been able to make out the entire legend, and have succeeded moreover in referring every word to its correspondent in the Persian original. Mr. Tasker, far more adventurous than Westergaard, descended by ropes from the summit of the cliff, and took his copy of the writing swinging in mid-air. He remained indeed for several hours in this perilous position during five successive days, in order to secure for his work the utmost available accuracy.

classify the dynasties and furnish the means of identifying the kings,—
how can it be supposed, that with all the difficulties that beset, and none
of the facilities that assist Egyptologers, two or three individuals are to
accomplish in a couple of years, more than all Europe has been able to
effect in half a century? I have thought it necessary to make these
observations, in order to put the Society on its guard against running
away with an idea, that the philological branch of the Assyrian
inquiry has been exhausted; and that nothing now remains but to
read inscriptions and reap the fruits of our knowledge. A commencement has been made; the first outwork has been carried in a hitherto
impregnable position—and that is all. I will now state exactly what
we know of the language.

The Babylonian translations of the Persian text in the trilingual
tablets, including, of course, the long Inscription at Nakhsh-i-Rustam
and the fragments from Behistun[1], have furnished a list of about two
hundred Babylonian words, of which we know the sound approximately, and the meaning certainly. These words are almost all found
either in their full integrity, or subjected to some slight modification,
in Assyrian, and we can usually, by their means, arrive at a pretty
correct notion of the general purport of the phrase in which they
occur. The difficult, and at the same time the essential part of the
study of Assyrian, consists in thus discovering the unknown from the
known, in laying bare the anatomy of the Assyrian sentences, and,
guided by grammatical indications, by a few Babylonian landmarks,
and especially by the context, in tracing out, sometimes through
Semitic analogies, but more frequently through an extensive comparison of similar or cognate phrases, the meaning of words which
are otherwise strange to us. It is in this particular branch of the
study, which I have prosecuted with great diligence and with all
available care, that I think I have made good progress, having added
about two hundred meanings certainly, and one hundred more probably, to the vocabulary already obtained through the Babylonian
translations. I estimate the number of words which occur in the
Babylonian and Assyrian Inscriptions at about five thousand, and I
do not pretend to be acquainted with more than a tenth part of that
number; but it must be remembered, that the five hundred known

[1] Many of the standard expressions at Behistun, such as "the rebels having
assembled their forces came against me offering battle; I fought with them and
defeated them, &c., &c.," prove to have been adopted almost verbatim from the
Assyrian annals. It was, indeed, the discovery of known passages of this sort in
the Obelisk Inscription, that first gave me an insight into the general purport of
the legend,

words constitute all the most important terms in the language, and are in fact, sufficient for the interpretation of the historical Inscriptions, and for the general recognition of the object of every record, be it an invocation or dedication, or, as it more frequently happens, be it intended as a mere commemorative legend.

The next subject to be considered, is the actual language of the Assyrian and Babylonian Inscriptions, a language which is certainly neither Hebrew, nor Chaldee, nor Syriac, nor any of the known cognate dialects, but which, nevertheless, presents so many points of analogy with those dialects, both in grammatical structure and in its elemental words, that it may, I think, be determinately classed among the Semitic family. It will be observed, that I here include the languages of Assyria and Babylonia in a common category. They can hardly be termed identical, inasmuch as each dialect affects the employment of certain specific verbal roots, and certain particular nouns and adjectives; but they are at any rate sufficiently alike in their internal organization to render illustrations drawn from the Inscriptions of Babylon applicable to those of Assyria, in so far as such illustrations may be of philological value. Although, therefore, the examples which I am about to cite are chiefly taken from the Babylonian translations at Behistun, the Semitic affinities which they indicate may be understood to be all more or less shared by the Assyrian.

One of the peculiarities of Babylonian, and which must be carefully borne in mind in tracing etymologies, is, that the powers of *l* and *v*, when occurring as the complement of a syllable, and sometimes even as initial articulations, are almost undistinguishable; this interchange being the same that led the Phœnicians to write *Malik* and *Mók* indifferently[1], that softened the Hebrew הלך, "to go," into הוך in Chaldee; that has, in fact, induced the French universally to substitute *u* for the silent *l* of other languages, as in "*autre*" for *alter*, "*faux*" for *falsus*, "*chaud*" for *calidus*, &c., &c.

There is thus a definite article in Babylonian, frequently, but by no means invariably employed, which we may read *hav;* this article standing halfway, as I think, between the Berber *va* and the Coptic Π on the one side, and the Hebrew *hal* and Arabic *Al* on the other[2].

[1] See Gesen. Monum. Phœnic., vol. I., p. 431.

[2] The true, or at any rate the primitive pronunciation of the Bab. article, which is also used as a demonstrative pronoun and adverb, may perhaps be *halv* or *harv*. Compare the Chaldee אלו or ארו, and see Gesenius's remarks on this word in page 84 of his Lexicon. Some of the forms of the article are,

In the Babylonian adjectives and nouns, a final *t* marks the feminine gender. The masculine forms its plural in *m*, *n*, and *t*, indifferently, thus fluctuating between Hebrew, Chaldee, and Arabic, and being also allied to the Coptic and Egyptian inflexion in ⲟⲩ. The true feminine plural ending seems to be *át*, but the distinction of gender is by no means rigidly observed; and moreover, as ideographs or monograms are frequently employed to mark these grammatical conditions, it is by no means easy to determine the pronunciation of the different forms.

I do not think that the construct state was marked by any orthographical change, or in fact, that there was any indication of a noun being placed "in regimine," beyond its being attached to the preceding noun by the relative *sha* or *da*. Other undoubted Semitic characteristics, however, are the formation of the abstract noun by the addition of *ut* to the primitive form, as in the words *arkut*, "kingdom," *galut*, "slavery[1]," &c.; the occurrence of verbal nouns formed by prefixing *t*, as *takhaz*, "battle," from אחד, "to join together;" participial nouns, such as *Nikrut*, "the rebels," from the Niphal form of *kar*, "to revolt;" *mattet* for *mattenet*, "gifts" or "tribute," from *ten*, "to give," &c., &c.

The pronouns, however, are the most interesting of all the parts of speech, and are generally made use of as the touchstones of language. I shall examine them therefore in some detail.

The 1st personal pronoun of the sing. number in Bab. and Assyr. is *anak*, closely resembling the Egyptian *Anok*, and Hebrew *Anokhi;* suffixed to nouns it is *uá* and *i*, to verbs *ani;* there are also two separate forms of the 1st person used with particles in a possessive, dative, ablative, and instrumental sense; they are *tuwa* and *ettuwa*, and are not clearly distinguishable. They are of course allied to the Coptic pronominal suffix of the 1st person, *ti*, and also to the prætérite sufformatives of the 1st person, *ti* in Hebrew, *tu* in Arabic.

Achæm. ⟨cuneiform⟩ : Assyrian ⟨cuneiform⟩; ⟨cuneiform⟩; &c. : Babylonian, perhaps, ⟨cuneiform⟩; ⟨cuneiform⟩, &c., but of these last I am not at all certain.

[1] I may here observe, that my reason for reading the abbreviated monogram ⟨cuneiform⟩, signifying "a king," as "*arko*" is, that at Behistun the word is always written at length ⟨cuneiform⟩, which can only be, I think, *Ar k a u=arko*. The other monogram ⟨cuneiform⟩, which has the full phonetic power of *men*, may very possibly stand for *melik*.

The pronoun of the 2nd pers. sing. in its separate form occurs only in one passage, and there it appears to be *nanta*, but the orthography is doubtful, and it may possibly be *anta*. Suffixed it is to be recognized everywhere as a simple *k*, an essential Semitic form.

The 3rd pers. sing. masc. is *su*, which is certainly the same as the Hebrew and Arabic *hu* or *huwa*, and suffixed either to verbs or nouns, it is usually *s*. The feminine personal pronoun I have not been able yet to identify, for notwithstanding all the Greek gossiping about the ladies of Assyria and Persia, in their records and sculptures the kings of those countries seem to have eschewed all notice of the female sex with true Oriental jealousy. As an affixed personal pronoun, the *s* seems in Assyrian and Babylonian to have answered equally for the masc. and fem. gender, whereas in Egyptian, it was applicable exclusively to the latter.

In the plural number I have not met with the pronoun of the 1st pers. used separately, but affixed it is *huni*, and with a possessive sense *etteni*, evidently the Coptic *ten*. The 2nd person plur. is also wanting; but the 3rd pers. plur. occurs very commonly, and is strictly African. In its separate form it is *ússen*, as in Saho, and suffixed it is *sen* for the masc., and *sent* for the feminine, forms which are very like Egyptian, and absolutely identical with the Berber. I observe, however, an instance of inflexion in the pronoun of the 3rd person, which is hardly reconcilable with Semitic usage. *Ussen* in the dative or accus. case, either takes a particle before, or an inflexion after it; that is, "for them" or "to them" *an ussen* and *ussen-at* are used indifferently, and sometimes even we have *senat* and *senut*[1].

Among the demonstrative pronouns we have for "this," *haga*[2] masc., *hagát* fem., and in the plur. *hagnit* or *hannit*. *Hagá*, I must add, is the Babylonian form of the Hebrew הזה, the sibilant being hardened to a guttural; and *haza*, again, by a further change, becomes in Arabic هٰذَا. Curiously enough, however, in Pushtoo, the Babylonian *haga* is found perfectly unaltered. The remote demonstrative pronoun "that," is *annut* or *allut*, the liquids, as I have before mentioned, interchanging; and although there is no exact representative of this term in Hebrew or Chaldee, there are many cognate forms, as אֵלֶּה, הֵנָּה, &c.

[1] These pronouns occur repeatedly at Behistun and Nakhsh-i-Rustam, and the forms used are precisely the same as we find in the earliest inscriptions of Assyria.

[2] It will thus be seen that the letter ⟨cuneiform⟩ or ⟨cuneiform⟩, which has been a stumbling-block to all previous inquirers, is a hard guttural,

I have now to consider the verbs.

In the present stage of our Babylonian knowledge, I cannot pretend to classify the verbal conjugations. They are, however, undoubtedly very numerous, and appear to be used almost indiscriminately. I recognize, I think, independently of those which may be formed by a permutation of the interior vowels, and which, owing to the want of points, it is impossible to discriminate, the Niphal, Hiphil or Hophal, and Hithpael of the Hebrew, together with the Chaldee Ithpaal, Aphel, Ittaphal, Shaphel, and Ishtaphel. There are also, I think, some of the more unusual conjugations which are found in Arabic and Amharic.

In one remarkable particular, however, the Babylonian verb varies from the usage of all other Semitic languages; it marks a distinction of persons by prefixes instead of suffixes[1]. The 1st person thus always commences with an *ă* or *ĕ*; the 2nd apparently with *t*, and the 3rd with the long or short *i*, the theme being otherwise unchanged. In the plural, *ni* is prefixed for the 1st person; the 2nd person is used too rarely to admit of a rule being established; and in the 3rd person plural alone is there a suffix, which suffix, moreover, being a simple *n*, is, I think, the characteristic of number rather than of person. It may be understood, that these personal affixes are exceedingly liable to be confounded with the conjugational characteristics, and moreover, as there are no vowel points, that it is often impossible to say what conjugation may be used. A still greater difficulty exists in distinguishing between the past and the present tenses. I can hardly believe that the Babylonians did not recognize a distinction of time in the verb, (although the frequent employment of the present after the *wav* of conversion in Hebrew with a præterite sense, would seem of itself to indicate a certain want of precision on this point); yet, it is certain that there is but one general form of conjugating the verbal roots in Babylonian, according to persons, and that this form is used indifferently for the past and present tenses of the Persian translation[2].

The Babylonian, like all Semitic tongues, is rich in particles, although

---

[1] I am here alluding especially to the past tense, which in Hebrew and Arabic is considered to be the root of the verb. In the present tense, those languages, it must be admitted, prefix the personal characteristic, as in Babylonian, and make use indeed of the same, or nearly the same prefixes, to denote the different persons.

[2] This confusion of time may, perhaps, be considered to corroborate Mr. Garnett's explanation of the Semitic verb, as a mere abstract noun in combination with oblique personal pronouns.

it sometimes employs the same term in a great variety of senses; for instance, the forms *an*, *en*, and *in*, which are certainly closely allied, and which are used almost indifferently, express the sense of, "to," "for," "in," "by," "with," and are further employed to individualize the noun, like the Hebrew את, and Chaldee ית, which are generally considered to mark the object of the verb, or, as we are accustomed to say, the accusative case[1].

I have not determined a great number of Assyrian and Babylonian adverbs, but those which I have found, are either formed immediately from pronominal themes, or they are compounded with prepositions, as in Hebrew. The adverbs of negation are, *al*, *lá*, and *yán*, which are all strictly Semitic. The conjunctions in common use are, for "and," and "also," *u*, *va*, and *at*. The two first are common to all the Semitic tongues; the last may, perhaps, be compared with the Latin "*et*."

The observations which I have thus made, although necessarily brief and superficial, as they relate to those particular characteristics by which philologists are now agreed the type of a language should be tested, may be considered sufficient to establish the determinate classification of Babylonian and Assyrian as Semitic dialects; but it is not only in organization and grammatical structure that analogies may be traced between these languages on the one side, and Hebrew, Chaldee, and Coptic on the other. There is also a very great resemblance in the vocabulary; that is, in the roots and stem words, which, next to the machinery for expressing the relations of time, place, person, number, gender, and action, are the most important aids to the identification of the lingual type.

The following examples will fully bear out this assertion, and will moreover show, that as vowel sounds are now admitted to be of secondary developement, and of no real consequence in testing the element of speech, the roots are almost universally biliteral; the Babylonian and Assyrian being thus found in a more primitive state than any other of the Semitic dialects of Asia open to our research, inasmuch as the roots are free from that subsidiary augment which in Hebrew, Aramæan, and Arabic has caused the triliteral to be usually regarded as the true base, and the biliteral as the defective one.

---

[1] Other Babylonian particles of undoubted Semitic origin are, *lipenai*, "before;" *itta*, "with;" *ad*, "to;" *anog*, "in front of," &c. Compound prepositions are also extensively used both in Assyrian and Babylonian.

Guv, "to say;" a form which connects the Arabic قَال with the Persian گو or گَف, or Sans. Gup, through the Babylonian *v*[1].

Ten, "to give;" comp. Hebrew נתן, "to give;" Greek δοω; Sans. *da;* Lat. "dono;" Egypt. *ti, taa, tei, to, &c.*

Ar, "to be," or "become;" this is Egyptian.

Duk, "to smite," or "kill;" Heb. דקק, "to beat small;" Arab. دقّ used exactly like the Bab. verb.

Rak, "to go over;" comp. Hebrew רגע, "to divide;" Arab. رجع "to return."

Mit, "to die;" מות in Heb.; مات in Arab.

Rad, "to go down;" comp. ירד in Heb.; ورد in Arab.

Tá and *bá*, "to come;" comp. אתה and בוא.

Ru, "to go;" *ruh*, in vulgar Arab.; and the same in the Arian languages.

El, "to go up," or "ascend;" עלה in Heb.; and على in Arab.

Ber, "to cross over;" *ibar* in Heb. and Arab.

Lak, "to reach;" comp. Arab. لقى

Kun, "to appoint," "establish," or "do;" כון in Heb.; and allied, I think, with the Pers. كن

Tseb, "to set up," or "fix;" comp. נצב ,יצב in Heb.; and نصب in Arab.

Sib, "to dwell;" Heb. ישב.

Men, "to allot;" Heb. מנה.

A number of other roots are not so immediately to be recognized, but are all probably more or less connected with Semitic forms. Such as *bes*, "to do," or "make;" *ver*, "to see;" *kher*, "to receive;" *sar*, "to go out;" *kem*, "to take away;" *bám*, "to arise;" *raz*, "to lie," or "deceive;" *kar*, "to rebel;" *bar*, "to send;" *zat*, "to seize," &c.

---

[1] As a further proof of the identity of the Arabic قَال "to say," with the Bab. *guv*, it may be observed, that the same form answers in the Inscriptions for the word "all," which is כל or كل, thus almost determinately connecting the *l* and *v*, and affording another example of the interchange of the gutturals.

The following nouns also may be of interest.

Et, "a father;" comp. *etf* in Egypt.; *Ata,* Turkish; Lat. *At-avus*[1].

Am, "a mother;" the same in Heb. and Arab.

Bar, "a son;" the exact Syriac form.

Arko or *eneko,* "a king;" comp. the Greek αναξ[2]; Lat. *rex;* "*neg,*" in Ethiopian, "to rule;" whence Negus, &c., &c.; Armen. *arkai;* and perhaps Egypt. *erro;* the name Abednego may thus mean the same as *Abdulmalik,* "the slave of the king."

Beth, "a house;" *Ir,* "a city;" *bar,* "the earth;" *erts,* "land;" *sem,* "a name;" *raba,* "great;" *itsiv,* "faithful;" *hem,* "a day," for *yam; sekeb,* "a cross;" for *seleb;* all these being closely allied to the Hebrew and Arabic; others approach more nearly to the African.

Tahv, "a mountain;" Cop. ⲦⲀⲨ.

Sar, "a brother;" Cop. ⲤⲀⲚ.

Ter or *H-ter,* "a horse;" completely Egyptian.

In selecting these examples from the numerous lists which I have collected of Babylonian and Assyrian vocables, I have merely wished to give such a general view of those languages as may decide the question of their lingual type. For all those details of alphabetical structure, of grammatical relation, and of etymology, upon which depends the authenticity of the readings that I shall presently communicate to the Society, I must refer to the Memoir which I have for many years been employed in preparing for publication, and which will be printed in the Society's Journal with all convenient despatch[3].

---

[1] In the term *etua,* which occurs so frequently in the trilingual inscriptions, the termination is the pronominal suffix of the 1st person, used independently of the possessive pronoun signifying "my."

[2] αναξ is for *a-nac-s,* as *rex* is for *rec-s, nac* and *rec* being the stem-words; it is this positive identity of the *n* and *r* in the cognate forms, which makes me doubt whether ⟨⟨ *n* may not stand for *eneko,* as ▷▷▷ *r* for *arko,* rather than retain its full phonetic power of *men,* as an abbreviation of *melik.*

[3] I also wish to be understood, that in giving these examples, I do not consider myself pledged to their definite phonetic rendering. I have neither adopted, nor do I conceive it possible to adopt, any system with regard to the employment of the vowels in Assyrian and Babylonian, and no great dependence therefore can be placed on the appearance of the word in the Roman character.

I now proceed to an examination of the Inscriptions. The discoveries of Mr. Layard and M. Botta are no doubt so well and so generally known, that in naming the Assyrian ruins, in order to identify the inscriptions appertaining to the different localities, I shall be sufficiently understood. As a preliminary step, however, and in order to avoid confusion, I must correct the nomenclature by which these ruins are usually designated. Nimrud, the great treasure-house which has furnished us with all the most remarkable specimens of Assyrian sculpture, although very probably forming one of that groupe of cities, which, in the time of the prophet Jonas, were known by the common name of Nineveh, has no claim itself, I think, to that particular appellation. The title by which it is designated on the bricks and slabs that form its buildings, I read doubtfully as Levekh[1], and I suspect this to be the original form of the name which appears as Calah in Genesis, and Halah in Kings and Chronicles[2], and which indeed, as the capital of Calachene, must needs have occupied some site in the immediate vicinity[3]; and I may add, that before I had deciphered the name of the city on the slabs of Nimrud, this geographical identification was precisely that at which I had arrived, from observing that the Samaritan version of the Pentateuch employs for the Hebrew Calah the term Lachisa, a form which Babylonian orthography shows

---

[1] The name is written indifferently ⊨𝍩 ⊢𝍩, ⊨𝍩 ◁ and ⊨𝍩 𝍩⊲; and the initial character which is thus common to all the forms, is one unfortunately regarding which I still entertain some doubt. Its complete syllabic power is, I think, *l-v*, (or, which would be the same thing in Assyrian, *r-m*,) but it also appears very frequently to represent one only of these sounds, and whether this curtailment may be the effect of that resolution of the syllable into its component literal powers to which I have already alluded, or whether it may be owing to the homogeneity of the *l* and *v*, is a point which I cannot yet venture to decide. Such, indeed, is the laxity of alphabetical expression in Assyrian, that even if the true power of ⊨𝍩 were proved to be *L-v*, I could still understand ⊨𝍩 ◁ being pronounced Halukh.

[2] See Gen. x. 11.; 2 Kings xviii. 11.; 1 Chron. v. 26.

[3] It has been asserted that the Calachene of the Greeks was exclusively a mountain district; but I cannot see any sufficient grounds for that geographical restriction. Strabo (Lib. XVI., *ad init.*) in describing Assyria, classes together τὰ περὶ τὸν Νῖνον πεδία, Δολομηνή τε, καὶ Καλαχηνὴ, καὶ Χαζηνὴ, καὶ Ἀδιαβηνὴ, all these applying certainly to the low country between the mountains and the Tigris. In another passage, also, he says, ἕως τῆς Καλαχηνῆς, καὶ τῆς Ἀδιαβηνῆς, ἔξω τῶν Ἀρμενιακῶν ὅρων, (Lib. XI., p. 770,) thereby positively excluding Calachene from the mountains. Ptolemy, also, when he says that Calacine lies *above* Adiabene, means perhaps to the north of it.

to be absolutely the same as the Greek name Larissa[1], by which
Xenophon designated the great ruined capital that was passed by the
Ten Thousand[2], a few miles to the northward of the Lycus[3]. The real
and primitive Nineveh, which is frequently mentioned in the inscriptions, and which appears to have been the proper seat of Assyrian
royalty, I conjecture to have occupied the site where we now see the
huge mound opposite to Mosul, surmounted by the pretended tomb of
the prophet Jonas; for we have historical proof of this particular
mound having been locally termed Nineveh, from the time of the
Arab conquest down to comparatively modern times[4]; and I think,
moreover, we may gather from the inscriptions, that the ruins
a short distance to the northward, which are now termed Koyunjik,
were not the true Nineveh itself, but formed a suburb of that capital[5].
The proper name by which Koyunjik was known I have not yet
been able to make out upon the bricks, but under one form it would
seem to resemble the title Mespila, by which Xenophon designated the
ruins; and if such should ultimately prove to be the case, it will furnish
us with an explanation of the Greek historian's silence on the subject

---

[1] Michaelis noticed the Samaritan לקסה in his Spicilegium, p. 247, but
failed to recognize its identity with Larissa, though he must have remembered
that Eusebius writes Χαβατσσοαράχο; for the Λαβοροσοάρχος of Josephus.

[2] Ἀφίκοντο ἐπὶ τὸν Τίγρητα ποταμόν· ἐνταῦθα πόλις ἦν ἐρήμη, μεγάλη,
ὄνομα δ' αὐτῆς Λάρισσα.—Xen. Anab., Lib. III., C. 4. 6—12.

[3] The Jerusalem Targum and Jonathan translate the Calah of Genesis, by
Hadith, חדית, a name which, owing to careless transcription and vicious punc-
tuation, has usually been read Parioth or Harioth. Hadith, however, or "the
New," is the name of a large town in the immediate vicinity of Nimrud, built
under the Sassanians, and restored by Merwan Ibn Mahommed, one of the earliest
Arab leaders; and it was certainly, I think, in allusion to this place, that the
Chaldee interpreters substituted חדית for כלח. See Yacût's Lexicon, *in voce*
حديثة.

[4] The forts of Ninawi to the east, and of Mosul to the west of the Tigris, are
mentioned in the accounts of the campaigns of Abdullah Ibn Mo'etemer, in
A.H. 16, and of 'Otbeh Ibn Farkad, in A.H. 20. See Ibn Athir, quoting from
Beladheri, in the annals of those years.

[5] The name of Nineveh occurs upon most of the Koyunjik bricks, but it is
united with a qualifying epithet, which denotes, I think, the particular northern
suburb, and of which I have never yet met with a fair and legible impress. That
Koyunjik can hardly be the true and original capital, I gather from the certainty
we possess of its having been built by the son of the Khorsabad king, whilst
Nineveh, under both its forms, ⌖ and ⌖, is fre-
quently mentioned as the royal residence, in the Inscriptions of the Obelisk king,
who lived perhaps a century earlier.

of Nineveh[1]. The suburb, in fact, having outgrown the original capital before the extinction of the empire, may have conferred its own name of Mespila for a time on the whole mass of ruins; while in the end, antiquity may, as is so often the case, have re-asserted its right, and thus revived the ancient and indigenous title of Nineveh. Up to the present time excavations have not been attempted on this site,—the spot, indeed, is so much revered by the Mohammedans, as the supposed place of sepulture of the prophet Jonas, that it is very doubtful if Europeans will be ever permitted to examine it. Mr. Layard, however, will hardly leave Assyria without securing some specimens from the site, and these will be at any rate sufficient to decide the question of nomenclature.

The only other site, which it is at present necessary to mention, is Khorsabad, or, as it has been sometimes termed, the French Nineveh. This city, although an immediate dependency of Nineveh, had also a particular title, being called after the king who founded it. I cannot determinately read the king's name,—in fact, the name, in common with most others, had not, I think, any determinate or uniform phonetic rendering; but, under one of its forms, it may very well read Sargon, which we know from Isaiah to have been a name in use among the Assyrian monarchs, and which, singularly enough, is the actual designation applied by the early Arab geographers to the ruins in question[2].

Having thus distinguished the four localities of Nimrud or Halah, Nebbi Yunus or Nineveh, Koyunjik or Mespila, and Khorsabad or

---

[1] It seems to me, at the same time, very possible, that Xenophon's name of Mespila may denote Mosul, and not Nineveh. He says the Greeks encamped, πρὸς τεῖχος ἔρημον μέγα, πρὸς τῇ πόλει κείμενον, ὄνομα δ' ἦν τῇ πόλει Μέσπιλα, and we may very well understand the description which follows of the ruins to apply to the τεῖχος ἔρημον μέγα, "the great deserted inclosure," rather than to Mespila. If Xenophon, indeed, had forgotten the name of the ruins, nothing would have been more natural than for him to illustrate the position by a reference to the neighbouring city; and that the name of Mosul, which so very much resembles Mespila, is far more ancient than the Mohammedan period to which it has been usually assigned, can be proved, I think, from a variety of sources.

[2] Yacút, quoting from some unknown ancient author, speaks of Khurstabadh, خرستابانة, as a village east of the Tigris, opposite to Mosul, among the dependencies of Nineveh, and adjoining the old ruined city of Sarghun, (written صرعون for صرغون), where treasure to a large amount had been found by excavating. It was I believe this very passage of Yacút, well known to the Mohammedan doctors, which led the Turkish authorities, in the first instance, to watch M. Botta's proceedings with so much jealousy and mistrust.

Sargon, I proceed to consider the Assyrian history. Our materials
are, I regret to say, as yet of so limited and fragmentary a nature,
that, however they may be calculated to awaken interest, or even to
stimulate inquiry, they can yield, in their present shape, as far at any
rate as chronology is concerned, no positive results.

It must be remembered that not only is the system of the Assyrian
writing in the last degree obscure, and the language in which the
writing is expressed, unintelligible, except through the imperfect key
of the Behistun translations, and the faint analogies of other Semitic
tongues, but that even if all the tablets hitherto discovered were
as certainly to be understood as the memorials of Greece and Rome,
we should still be very far indeed from possessing a connected history
of the Assyrian empire.   We have, it is true, several valuable records
of particular kings, and we are able, in some instances, to work out a
genealogical series to the extent of at least six generations, but such
notices go but a very little way in filling up the long period of nine
centuries which must have intervened between the first institution of
the Assyrian monarchy and the final destruction of Nineveh, at the
commencement of the sixth century before the Christian era.   Until
we shall discover something like epochal dates, either civil or astro-
nomical, or until we shall have a complete royal list, extending from
the commencement of the dynasty to some king mentioned either in
sacred or profane history, whose era may thus furnish us with a
starting-place, it will be in vain to hope to arrive at anything like a
determinate chronology.   All that we can do at present is to infer,
from the internal evidence afforded by the inscriptions, the relative
position of the different royal families, and the interval of time that
may have elapsed between them; while, for anything like positive
chronology, we are dependent on a process of induction still more
feebly supported, and on collateral testimony still less susceptible of
proof.   I am certainly not wedded myself to any particular system
or any particular authority; but that the Nimrud marbles are of
a very high antiquity, far more ancient than the historic period of
the Assyrian empire, to which they have been sometimes assigned, I
cannot reasonably doubt.   Comparing together, indeed, all the various
sources of evidence that can be brought to bear upon the subject, and,
relying principally on the indications of political geography, which
it will be seen in the sequel the inscriptions themselves afford, the
conviction has been almost forced on me that the era of the building
of the north-west palace at Halah or Nimrud, which, as far as art
is concerned, was certainly the most flourishing period of the
Assyrian empire, and soon after which its political power also pro-

bably reached its culminating point, must have followed very closely on the extinction of the nineteenth dynasty of Egypt; the institution of the Assyrian monarchy thus pretty well synchronising with the Argive colonization of Greece and with the first establishment of the Jews in Palestine. At any rate we cannot, I think, be far wrong in assigning the greater portion of the Assyrian marbles that adorn our Museum, and particularly the famous black obelisk bearing the inscription which I shall presently translate, to the twelfth, or at earliest to the thirteenth century before the Christian era. I shall recur again to the chronological question, after I have given a précis of the contents of the inscriptions, and shall then succinctly state the grounds on which I have assumed this approximate date.

The earliest records that have been yet brought to light, written in the Cuneiform character, are certainly the inscriptions of the north-west Palace of Nimrud; these belong to a king, whose name I read as Assar-adan-pal, and whom I am inclined to identify with the Sardanapalus of the Greeks; not the voluptuary of historical romance, but the warlike Sardanapalus of Callisthenes[1], whose place of sepulture, marked by an enormous tumulus, Amynthas, an ancient Greek author, quoted by Athenæus, notices at the gate of the Assyrian capital[2]. This tomb, I may add, which is in all probability the great Pyramid of Nimrud now being opened by Mr. Layard, was popularly supposed to have been erected by Semiramis over the remains of Ninus, and was thus usually placed at Nineveh instead of Halah; but Xenophon, the only eye-witness whose account has come down to us, correctly described the tumulus as the most striking feature among the ruins of Larissa, which was the name by which Halah was then known[3].

But although this Sardanapalus, the builder of the north-west Palace of Nimrud, is the earliest Assyrian monarch whose annals have been

---

[1] As quoted by Suidas, in voce Σαρδανοπαλ.

[2] Amynthas, it is true, considers this capital to be Nineveh, and his historical authority is still further vitiated by his ascribing the capture of the city to Cyrus instead of Cyaxares; but at the same time, as he was a professed geographer, his statement is of value, that the tomb of Sardanapalus was in Assyria, and not in Cilicia, as the later Greeks unanimously believed. See Athen. Deip., lib. xii. c. 7.

[3] The words of Xenophon are, Παρ' αὐτὴν τὴν πόλιν ἦν πυραμὶς λιθίνη, τὸ μὲν εὖρος ἑνὸς πλέθρου, τὸ δὲ ὕψος δύο πλέθρων. Anab., lib. iii. c. 4. s. 11. The account given of this Mausoleum by Diodorus, quoting from Ctesias, is also very striking, but the value of the notice is destroyed by the geographical blunder of placing Nineveh on the Euphrates. Ovid alludes to the same spot under the name of "Busta Nini," in his story of Pyramus and Thisbe, though, with a poet's license, he transfers the locality to Babylon.

yet discovered, it does not by any means follow that he was the first
founder of the city of Halah, still less that he was the first great
builder in Assyria, or the first king who ruled over the land.   On the
contrary, it is an ascertained fact, that Sardanapalus did not stand
nearly at the head of his line.   Assyrian civilization, as exemplified
in the Nimrud sculptures, could not, of course, have sprung full-grown
from the womb of time.   There must needs have been, as in Egypt, a
long course of careful training, to have brought the inhabitants of the
valley of the Tigris to that state of proficiency in the arts of life
which is indicated by the monuments that have lately been disinterred,
and in all probability, therefore, several dynasties ruled over Assyria
anterior to that family which numbered the first Sardanapalus among
its ranks.   Of such dynasties, it is true, if we except the doubtful
classifications of Alexander Polyhistor, and the still more suspicious
lists of Ctesias and the chronologers, no historical traces whatever
remain to us.   There are no materials at present available to show
how, where, or when, the civilization of Assyria was effected.   The
inscriptions do not even furnish any certain evidence as to the period
at which the ancestors of Sardanapalus first attained kingly power;
but still the names of several kings are either directly or indirectly
mentioned; and these notices prove that a flourishing monarchy must
have existed in the valley of the Tigris long anterior to the age of
the Nimrud palace.

Sardanapalus, indeed, in every one of his inscriptions names both
his father and his grandfather, and applies to each of them the title of
" King of Assyria."   In commemorating, moreover, the building of the
palace at Nimrud, he speaks of a still earlier king, Temen-bar I., who
was the original founder of the city of Halah.   I cannot positively fix
the interval between Temen-bar I. and Sardanapalus; in the Standard
Inscription, I have been sometimes induced to read the passage in
which the notice occurs, as " the stronghold of Halah, built by Temen-
bar, who was my third ancestor[1];" while the inscription of a later
king, which gives a sort of genealogical tree of the family, either
transposes the order of the father and grandfather of Sardanapalus, or,
breaking off the list at the latter king, it removes Temen-bar some
degrees higher up the line, and even names an earlier monarch, Bel-

---

[1] This passage occurs in line 15, of No. 1 of the British Museum series; from
a similar expression at Behistun, there can be no doubt but that the allusion is to
a precession of race, but I question very much if the sign ►┃┃┃ can here represent a number.

takat(?) who seems to have founded the kingdom[1]. Beyond, however, a mere string of titles difficult to understand, and possessing probably if understood, but little interest, we know nothing of these kings forming the early Assyrian succession, but the names. When I say, too, that we know the names, I merely mean that such names are recognizable wherever they occur; their definite phonetic rendering or pronunciation is a matter of exceeding difficulty, nay, as I think, of absolute impossibility; for, strange as it may appear, I am convinced that the early Assyrians did not distinguish their proper names by the *sound*, but by the *sense;* and that it was thus allowable, in alluding to a king by name, to employ synonyms to any extent, whether those synonyms were terms indifferently employed to denote the same deity, or whether they were different words used to express the same idea. This will be more easily understood as I proceed to notice the names. The title of Temen-bar is formed of two elements, Temen being the name of a god[2], which is, I believe, only met with in this proper name, and *bar* being perhaps the Hebrew בר, "beloved[3]." It would be allowable, according to the Assyrian usage, to represent this name by any words signifying "beloved of Temen;" and in reference to Temen-bar I., we do thus actually find the second element replaced by another monogram, which, although equivalent in sense, may possibly vary in sound[4].

The next king's name is, perhaps, Hemenk or Hevenk, which would seem to be the same as the Evechius of the Greeks, a title which the chronologers assert to have been the true Chaldean

---

[1] I refer to the Inscription of the second ⟨cuneiform signs⟩, published in Plate 70 of the British Museum series. I have not yet been able to assure myself of the meaning of the terms, nor the connexion of the clauses of this Inscription, but it seems quite impossible to reconcile the genealogical detail with the family notices contained in the legends of Sardanapalus and his son.

[2] This name might be read Deven as well as Temen. In fact, I consider the two forms to be identical in Assyrian.

[3] The second element of this king's name, which is usually written ⟨cuneiform sign⟩, may also possibly have the power of *Sver* or *Smer*, rather than simple *Bar*, as it represents the first syllable in the name of the Magian impostor, which was *Bardiya* in Persian, but Σμέρδις in Greek.

[4] In the Standard Nimrud Inscription the sign used is always ⟨cuneiform signs⟩, regarding the true phonetic power of which I am still in doubt; the genealogical inscription, however, No. 70, line 22, employs the same character, ⟨cuneiform sign⟩, which is used in the name of Temen-bar II., thus proving that the two titles are identical.

designation of Nimrud[1]. The explanation of this name, however, is even more doubtful than its pronunciation. If it be a compound, the first element will be *Hev* or *Hem*, a well-known Assyrian god, who, as his figure is usually accompanied on the cylinders
by a symbol representing " flame," may be supposed to be connected
with the Baal Haman of the Phœnician cippi, and the Hamánim or
" Sun images" on the altars of Baal, mentioned so frequently in Scripture[2]. It is possible, at the same time, that Hemenk or Hevenk may
have no connexion with *Hem*, but may be the name of a distinct
deity very rarely mentioned; for I find in one passage Hevenk
written exactly in the same manner, and called the father of Assarac[3],
the latter being the best known of all the members of the Assyrian
Pantheon.

The name of the third king signifies, as I think, " the servant of
Bar;" but it is quite impossible to give any definite form to the title;
for the word servant is rendered by terms differing as much from each
other as Abd and Khadim in Arabic; and Bar, moreover, is frequently replaced by Seb, these two names appertaining apparently
to be the same deity[4].

---

[1] The character ⟨glyph⟩, which interchanges with ⟨ or ⟨glyph⟩, as the initial
sign of this king's name, being used at Behistun for the first syllable of the name
of Imanish, may, I think, with some certainty be assigned the phonetic power of
—*m* or —*v*, and I consider it almost immaterial in Assyrian how we complete
the articulation. Where ⟨glyph⟩ however represents a god, as in this name, we
can never be sure that the phonetic power of the character is the value to be
attributed to the sign. ⟨glyph⟩ may be an abbreviation for *Khemosh*,
(comp. Heb. כמוש, and Polyhistor's name Χωμόσβηλος); or, ⟨, ⟨glyph⟩ and
⟨glyph⟩ may be ideographs for some god, whose name has not yet been phonetically identified. The homogeneity, indeed, of *m* and *v*, which are the true powers
of ⟨glyph⟩ and ⟨, is the chief argument I possess in favour of the phonetic
reading of the name. For the Greek Εὐήχιος, see Cory's Fragments, p. 67.

[2] Compare the Cylinders numbered 54, 58, 67, 133, &c., in Cullimore's
collection.

[3] I remarked this in an Inscription lately found at Koyunjik, which has not
yet been published.

[4] I conjecture that the abbreviation ⟨glyph⟩ *k*, or the more complete form
⟨glyph⟩ ⟨glyph⟩ *k, t,* or with the determinative prefixed, ⟨glyph⟩ ⟨glyph⟩ ⟨glyph⟩,
may represent the idea of " serving," the Assyrian term being perhaps cognate
with the first syllable of the Arabic root خدم ; and I further hazard an expla-

We now come to Sardanapalus, Assar-adan-pal, as I propose to read the three elements of which the name is composed[1]; and with this king commences our knowledge of the extent and power of the Assyrian monarchy.

In the north-west Palace of Nimrud there is an inscription of Sardanapalus repeated more than a hundred times; it contains a certain formula of royal commemoration, which, in regard to the titles employed, and the general character of the legend, was adopted by all succeeding kings of the dynasty in the dedication of their palaces.

It thus commences:—"This is the Palace of Sardanapalus, the nation of 𒀸 *ab* (?), which is also used for the first element of the name in place of 𒀸, as an abbreviation of *abd*. With regard to the second element of the name, supposing the true phonetic power of 𒁇 to be *Sver*, rather than *Bar*, as I generally render the sign, the variant monograms 𒁹 𒁹 or 𒁹 𒁹, might perhaps be referred to this actual title; the first, or *sb*, being an abbreviation of the name; and the second, *sr*, being pronounced *sur*, which would be phonetically equal to *Sver*. At the same time, I think it safer to suppose Bar, Seb, and Sur to denote the same god, than to assume the phonetic equivalence of the monograms. Possibly, indeed, 𒁹 which commences many names of gods, may be a distinct title, and the adjuncts may be qualifying epithets.

[1] I do not affect to consider this identification of the name of Sardanapalus as any thing more than a conjecture. The first element 𒀸, representing by abbreviation the god Assarac, and also commencing the name of Assyria, had, I think, the true phonetic power of *As-sar*, but if, as would appear probable from the indifferent employment of 𒁇 and 𒀸, the monogram should be here intended to denote the god, then a guttural must be introduced after Assar in pronouncing the king's name. The attribution again of the power of *adan* to the middle element, 𒁇 or 𒀸, is exceedingly doubtful. The only direct argument in its favour is that 𒀸, as the determinative of "a province," interchanges with 𒁇 or 𒀸, which has usually the phonetic value of *du*, while the adjunct 𒀸, I think, represents a terminal liquid, optionally softening to *u*. The last element, also, 𒁹 or 𒀸, I merely read as *pal*, from its appearing to have that power in the name of Nabopalassar, father of Nebuchadnezzar, as explained in note 2, p. 5. These few remarks upon the component parts of the Assyrian royal names will show the extreme difficulty of ascertaining their true pronunciation.

humble worshipper of Assarac[1] and Beltis[2], of the shining Bar[3], of
Ani[4], and of Dagon, who are the principal of the gods, the powerful and

---

[1] As I shall repeatedly have occasion to notice the god Assarac, I may as well
explain at once that I consider it to be almost certain that this name represents
the Biblical Nisroch, the god of the Assyrians, in whose temple Sennacherib was
slain. (2 Kings, c. xix. v. 37; and Isaiah, c. xxxvii. v. 38.) Whether the initial
N of the Hebrew name was an error of some ancient copyist, or a euphuism not
uncommon in Syriac, or whether it was not rather owing to the determinative for
a god, ⸺, which precedes the Cuneiform name, being read as a phonetic sign,
I will not pretend to decide; but it is worthy of remark that the Septuagint, who
wrote while the god in question was still probably worshipped on the banks of the
Tigris, and who may thus be supposed to have been familiar with the title,
replaced the Hebrew נסרך by 'Ασάραχ in one passage, and 'Εσοράχ in another.
That Assarac, moreover, was the true form of the Cuneiform name which was
usually expressed by the abbreviations ⸺ *as*, or ⸺ *a-sar*, or ⸺
as-sar, is rendered highly probable, by the full orthography which occurs in one
passage, (British Museum, No. 75, A. 1. 3,) of ⸺, the
title being there expressed with pure phonetic signs, while the epithet which is
added, of "father of the gods," would seem to establish the identity. Now it can
be shown by a multitude of examples occurring in the Assyrian Inscriptions, that in
early times the countries and cities of the East were very commonly named after
the gods who were worshipped there, or under whose protection the land was
believed to be. Assyria was thus certainly named after Assarac, the tutelar divinity of the nation, the geographical title being not only usually written in full,
Assarak or Assarah, but being sometimes also represented by the same abbreviated
monogram ⸺, which is used for the name of the god. The question then arises,
if the god Assarac, who imposed his own name on the country where he was worshipped, can be identified with the Biblical Ashur, who colonized Assyria. That
the Greeks (Xenocrates, quoted in the Etym. Mag. *in voce* 'Ασσυρία, and Eratosthenes, cited by Eustathius, ad Dionys. V. 775,) derived the name of Assyria
from a certain leader named 'Ασσωρ or 'Ασσύρ, I should not consider an argument
of much weight, for the heroes Armenus, Medus, and Perseus, after whom it was
pretended that the neighbouring provinces were named, were undoubtedly fabu-
lous: and the genealogies, moreover, recorded in the tenth chapter of Genesis, are
considered by an eminent authority to be nothing more than "an historical representation of the great and lengthened migrations of the primitive Asiatic race of
man," (Bunsen's Egypt, p. 182); but at the same time the double employment
of the Hebrew אשור and the Cuneiform ⸺ is certainly remarkable, and
there is no improbability in the Proto-patriarch of Assyria having been deified by
his descendants and placed at the head of their Pantheon. Assarac is named in
the Inscriptions "father of the gods;" "king of the gods;" "great ruler of the
gods," &c., and he would seem therefore to answer to the Chronos or Saturn,
whom the Greeks in their Assyro-Hellenic Mythology (conf. Paschal Chronicle:
John of Malala, &c.) made to be the husband of Semiramis or Rhea, the grand-

supreme ruler, the King of Assyria; son of '*the servant of Bar*[5],' the great king, the powerful and supreme ruler, King of Assyria; who was

father of Belus, and the progenitor of all the gods. Curiously enough, also, Beyer, who annotated Selden's work, "de Diis Syris," and who illustrated the Biblical notices of the Assyrian and Babylonian gods by references to the Talmud and the Rabbinical traditions, states (page 323) that Nisroch was considered to be iden- tical with the Greek Chronos or Saturn, thus confirming, on Jewish authority, the indication afforded by the epithets applied to Assarac in the incriptions. It has been assumed pretty generally in England, that the vulture-headed god, who is very frequently figured on the Nineveh marbles, must necessarily represent the Biblical Nisroch, *nasr* or *nisr* signifying " a vulture," both in Hebrew and Arabic, and the Zoroastrian oracle, Ὁ δὲ Θεός ἐστι κεφαλὴν ἔχων ἱέρακος, appearing to refer to the same Assyrian divinity. I cannot, however, at all subscribe to this doctrine. *Nisr*, " a vulture," can hardly by possibility have any etymological con- nexion with Assarac, which is the true orthography of the name of the Assyrian god. I do not indeed think that the vulture-headed figure is intended to represent any god, in the popular acceptation of that term. I should rather consider it to be an allegorical figure—a symbol, perhaps, connected with the philosophy of early Magism—of which the hidden meaning was known only to the priesthood. If Nisroch or Assarac is figured at all upon the Assyrian marbles, I should suppose him, as the head of the Pantheon, to be represented by that particular device of a winged figure in a circle, which was subsequently adopted by the Persians to denote Ormazd, the chief deity of their religious system. The Zoroastrian oracle of the hawk-headed god may, at the same time, very possibly refer to the Nimrud figure; for all the Zoroastrian Cabala, and in fact, the whole structure and machi- nery of Magism, as detailed in the Zend Avesta and Bun Dehesh, were derived, I think, from the later Chaldees; but I take the Theos of the oracle to be used altogether in an esoteric sense, and to have no connexion whatever with the primitive and vulgar mythology of Assyria.

[2] My reasons for supposing ►◄ to represent Beltis, are, 1stly, a common variant groupe for the deity in question is, ►►Ⴤ ►ⵏ ⴹⵟⵟⵟ, when ►ⵏ denotes *Bel*, and ⴹⵟⵟⵟ is, I think, a feminine characteristic, or at any rate an epithet applying exclusively to goddesses; 2ndly, the deity ►►Ⴤ ►ⵏ ⴹⵟⵟⵟ is sym- bolised on a cylinder, (see Cullimore's Cyl. No. 50) by a naked female figure nearly resembling the *Ken* of the Hieroglyphs; and 3rd, on the Obelisk, side 1, line 12, attached to ►►Ⴤ ►◄ is the epithet ⵟⵟⵟ Ⴤⵕⵕⵕ, " mother of the gods," ⵟⵟⵟ being used at Behistun for the Persian *mátá*.

[3] The epithet "*nero*," which I propose to render "shining," is applied to many of the gods; to Bel, to Bar, to Nebo (or Sut ?), even to Assarac; and it can hardly therefore be made use of as an argument in favour of the Sabæism of the Assyrian worship. It is probably the same word which occurs in the Biblical Nergal.

[4] The name of this deity is written indifferently ⵟⵟ ⵕⵕ or ⵟⵟ ⵕⵕ, but I have no clue to its identification in the general mythological system. At Khorsabad, Ani is usually joined with Ashtera, or the goddess Astarte.

[5] The usual phonetic form of this name is, perhaps, Kati-bar.

son of Hevenk[1], the great king, the powerful and supreme ruler, King of Assyria." After this introduction, the inscription goes on apparently to notice the efforts made by the king to establish the worship of the Assyrian gods generally throughout the empire, and, in connexion with this subject, incidentally as it were, occurs a list of the nations tributary to Nineveh, which is of considerable interest in affording the means of comparing the extent of the kingdom as it was constituted at that time, with the distribution given in later inscriptions, when the empire had been enlarged by conquest.

I am able neither to follow the sense throughout, nor even to read with any certainty some of the names, but I can still obtain a general insight into the geographical distribution. Firstly are mentioned the people of Nahiri (or Northern Mesopotamia[2]), of Lek (perhaps the Lycians before they moved to the westward), of Sabiri (the Sapires[3] ?), and of the plains sacred to the god Hem[4]. There is then an allusion to the countries beyond the river Tigris[5] as far as

---

[1] I may as well note that it is extremely doubtful if the middle character of this king's name really represent an *n*; I merely give it that power as I find ⊨𐌉, and ⊨𐌉𐌉 or ⊨𐌉𐌉𐌉, to interchange in the word for "man;" but there are equally strong grounds for classing ⊨𐌉 among the dentals; and the name in question therefore may very possibly read Hem-tak or Hem-tag.

[2] Nahiri frequently occurs as the name of a country about the head streams of the Tigris and Euphrates; it is, I think, the same as the Biblical ארם נחרים, and the Egyptian Naharaina; but I do not consider either of those names to apply to Mesopotamia, as that term was used by the Greek geographers.

[3] If this be the same name as the Khorsabad 𐎫𐎹 𐎹𐎹 𐎹𐎹𐎹, the allusion will be to a country lying between Armenia and Susiana, the Matiene, in fact, of Herodotus.

[4] The word which I doubtfully render "plains," is written 𐎹𐎹𐎹 𐎹 or 𐎹𐎹 𐎹𐎹𐎹 𐎹 or 𐎹𐎹 𐎹𐎹𐎹 𐎹𐎹 or 𐎹𐎹 𐎹𐎹𐎹, and is, I believe, identical with the Biblical ארם. Gesenius, it is true, translates Aram, "highlands," but this is hardly in accordance with the use of the term in Scripture; and I observe, moreover, in the last line of the Obelisk, the verb 𐎹𐎹𐎹𐎹 𐎹𐎹𐎹 𐎹𐎹𐎹, "I came down," in connexion with 𐎹𐎹 𐎹𐎹𐎹 𐎹, which would seem to show that the word must signify "low country" or "plains."

[5] The most ancient name of the Tigris was 𐎹𐎹 𐎹𐎹, of which I cannot venture to give the pronunciation. Its better-known appellation was Barseber, always written in Assyrian 𐎹𐎹 𐎹𐎹 𐎹𐎹, but with many variants in Hieratic and Cursive Babylonian. (Compare India-House Slab, col. 5, lines 15,

Syria[1]; and after the enumeration of several names not otherwise
known, there is a notice of the city of Rábek, which from many points
of evidence in the later inscriptions, I believe to represent Heliopolis,
the capital of Lower Egypt. In continuation I read, "I received
homage (?) from the nations on the river Sbenat, as far as Armenia[2];
from the plains of Larri to Ladsán; from the people beyond the
river Zab as far as the city of Tel Biari; from the city of Tel
Abtan to the city of Tel Zabdan; from the cities of Akrima and
Kharta, and the sea-coast dependent on Taha-Tanis, to the frontiers
of my country I brought abundance: from the plains of Bibad as far
as Tarmar, I bestowed (all) upon the people of my own kingdom[3]."

38, 45; col. 7, line 46, &c.; Bellino's Cylinder, col. 2, line 42; Rich, Pl. IX,

No. 4, l. 22.) The name of Dikel or Diglet, (Chaldee דיגלת, Arabic دجلة,

Diglito of Pliny,) however, was not unknown. At Behistun, 𒁹

is used in one passage for the more usual 𒁹, and I have
found the same title, but slightly varied in the spelling, in an Inscription of the
time of the Khorsabad king. See British Museum series, No. 65, l. 14, where the
phrase occurs, "I slew the Arab tribes who dwelt upon the Tigris."

[1] In some copies of this Inscription Syria is denoted by the capital city of the
Hittites, a city well known, under a slightly altered form, in the Inscriptions of the
Khorsabad period, and which I have been often tempted to read Shaluma, and to
identify with Jerusalem, (שלם or Σόλυμα): but generally, instead of this name,
𒁹 or 𒁹, we have the country of
𒁹, which is certainly, I think, the Lemenen or Remenen of
the Hieroglyphs, and which may very possibly be the Scriptural Lebanon. Comparing, indeed, the following passages in the British Museum series, Pl. 26, l. 16;
Pl. 39, l. 23; and Pl. 40, ls. 40 and 45, we can hardly doubt but that the three
names 𒁹, 𒁹 and 𒁹,
or *Lemenen, Hamana,* and *Serar,* refer to places immediately contiguous, and the
most reasonable explanation therefore certainly is, that they denote the great
mountain chain of Syria, the hills, in fact of Lebanon, Amana, and Shenir, which
are associated in the famous passage of Solomon's Song, c. iv. v. 8, and which are
otherwise well known in geography.

[2] Of the river Sbenat I know nothing, as it is not mentioned in any other
passage. The etymology, however, would seem to be Zend; compare *sventa,*
"holy." Armenia in this passage is sometimes named Ararat and sometimes
Aram Bedan, to the identification of which, unless it be the Padan Aram of
Scripture, I have no clue whatever.

[3] In this list the only remarkable place is Taha-Tanis, or, as it is may rather
perhaps be read, Taha-Dunis. This was a very celebrated city of Lower Chaldæa,

Now this list is no less remarkable for what it omits than what it mentions. It would seem as if the sea-coast of Phœnicia had not yet fallen under the power of Assyria, nor the upper provinces of Asia Minor—nor the high land of Media; and if Susiana and Babylonia were included in the empire, as the mention of Taha-Tanis would appear to indicate, they were not held of sufficient account to be noticed. Very different, it will be seen, was the condition of Assyria at a later epoch. The period when Phœnicia first came under the dominion of Assyria is fixed by a subsequent legend of Sardanapalus, which is inscribed upon the votive altar, as well as upon the Bull and Lion, which the king dedicated to his tutelary deity on returning from the Syrian campaign. In that inscription it is expressly stated, that while the king was in Syria he received the tribute of the kings of Tyre, and Sidon, of Acre, of Byblos, of Berytus, of Gaza, of Baiza (?), and of Aradus; a complete list being thus given of the great maritime cities of Phœnicia[1]. There is still another inscription of Sardanapalus and several detached fragments which are strictly and purely historical, being designed to illustrate the subject of the bas-reliefs to which they are attached. These pieces give succinct notices of the different wars in which the monarch was engaged, but they are all unfortunately in so mutilated a state, that a connected narrative cannot be obtained from them[2].

It will be of more interest then to pass on at once to Temen-bar II., the son of Sardanapalus, who built the centre palace at Nimrud, and of whose annals the Obelisk supplies us with a notice of singular completeness and detail. Comparing, indeed, the Obelisk Inscription with the writing upon the votive Bulls belonging to the Centre Palace, which were dedicated apparently at an earlier period of Temen-bar's reign, and with the legend on the statue found at Kileh Shergat, which was designed especially to commemorate the king's southern expe-

but I cannot identify the name in classical or Scriptural geography. I shall reserve all inquiry into the other names, the phonetic rendering of many of which is extremely doubtful, for the Memoir to be published hereafter.

[1] See British Museum series, Pl. 43, l. 10. The names of Tyre and Sidon, of Akarra (for the Heb. עֶכָּר, Greek Ἀκή, and modern Acre), of Gubal (Heb. גְּבָל, and Greek Βύβλος,) and Arvada (Heb. אַרְוַד, and Greek Ἀράδιοι) are certain; but the other three, which are moreover of very rare occurrence, are doubtful. In the Khorsabad Inscriptions, for Akarra or Acre is often substituted Maratha, which is of course the Μάραθος of Strabo, "πόλις ἀρχαία Φοινίκων," Lib. xvi. p. 518. As these sheets are passing through the press, I observe that Dr. Hincks has mistaken these Phœnician cities of Acre and Marath for the remote provinces of Aria and Parthia, provinces to which I am pretty sure the Assyrian arms never penetrated. See Khorsabad Inscriptions by Dr. Hincks, p. 31.

[2] See British Museum series, Plates 48 and 49.

dition, we have as complete a register of the chief events of the period as could well be desired.

Of this register, I will now accordingly undertake to give an explanation, merely premising that, although considerable difficulty still attaches to the pronunciation of the proper names, and although the meaning of particular passages is still unknown to me, I hold the accurate ascertainment of the general purport of the legend, to be no more subject to controversy than my decipherment of the Persian Inscriptions of Behistun[1].

The inscription on the Obelisk commences with an invocation to the gods of Assyria to protect the empire. I cannot follow the sense of the whole invocation, which takes up fourteen lines of writing, as well from the obscurity of the titles appertaining to the gods, as from the lacunæ in the text owing to the fracture of the corner edge of the gradines; but I perceive, I think, the following passages:—"The god Assarac, the great lord, king of all the great gods; Ani, the king; Nit, the powerful, and Artenk, the supreme god of the provinces[2]; Beltis, the protector, mother of the gods." A few lines further on we have "Shemir, (perhaps the Greek Semiramis) who presides over the heavens and the earth" (another god whose name is lost). "Bar," with an unknown epithet; then "- - - - Artenk, Lama, and Horus;" and after the interval of another line, "- - - - Tal, and Set, the attendants of Beltis, mother of the gods[3]." The favour of all these deities with Assarac at their head, the Supreme God of Heaven, is invoked for the protection of Assyria. Temen-bar then goes on to give his titles and genealogy; he calls himself, King of the Nations who worship Husi (another name for the god Shemir) and Assarac; King of Mesopotamia, (using a term which was afterwards particularly applied to the Euphrates[4]); son of Sardanapalus, the

---

[1] The claims here put forward require perhaps to be qualified, for I do not affect to consider my reading of the Obelisk Inscription in the light of a critical translation. Whenever, indeed, I have met with a passage of any particular obscurity I have omitted it, and the interpretation even which I have given of many of the standard expressions is almost conjectural. My object has been throughout to give a general idea of the nature of the Assyrian records, rather than to resolve particular difficulties of orthography or etymology.

[2] That the monogram ⯮⯭ denotes the goddess Nit, (Egyptian Neith ?), I infer from its being used at Behistun to express the last syllable in the name of king Nabunit, (Ναβόνιδος). Nit and Artank are named in the E. I. H. Insc., col. 4, l. 10.

[3] Most of these names are very doubtful indeed.

[4] The application to Assyria and Babylonia of the general name ⯮⯭ ⯭⯮, *Perrat*, seems to explain a passage in the Etym. Mag. Ἀσσυρία—ἡ Βαβυλωνία—τὸ μὲν πρῶτον ἐκαλεῖτο Εὐφράτις, ὕστερον δὲ Χαλδαῖα.

servant of Husi, the protector, who first introduced the worship of the gods among the many peopled nations (the exact terms being here used which answer to the "*dahyáwa paruwa-zana*" of Persepolis). Sardanapalus, too, is called the son of Katibar (or "the servant of Bar"), who was king of Zahiri, which seems to have been one of the many names of Assyria.

Temen-bar then says:—" At the commencement of my reign, after that I was established on the throne, I assembled the chiefs of my people and came down into the plains of Esmes, where I took the city of Haridu, the chief city belonging to Nakharni."

" In the first year of my reign, I crossed the Upper Euphrates, and ascended to the tribes who worshipped the god Husi. My servants erected altars (or tablets) in that land to my gods. Then I went on to the land of Khamána[1], where I founded palaces, cities, and temples. I went on to the land of Málar, and there I established the worship (or laws) of my kingdom."

" In the second year, I went up to the city of Tel Barasba, and occupied the cities of Ahuni, son of Hateni. I shut him up in his city, I then crossed the Euphrates, and occupied the cities of Dabagu and Abarta belonging to the Sheta, together with the cities which were dependent on them[2].

" In the third year, Ahuni, son of Hateni, rebelled against me, and having become independent, established his seat of government in the

---

[1] This name has many different forms, but wherever it occurs, it denotes, I think, Northern Syria, or rather perhaps the particular mountain ranges stretching from Cilicia to Libanus, being in fact the 'Αμάνος of the Greeks, and אמנה of Scripture. (See authorities in Bochart's Phaleg, col. 359.) The name should be pronounced Hamána or Amána, I think, in preference to the form I generally use of Khamána.

[2] The Sheta or Khita are repeatedly mentioned in the Egyptian Inscriptions of the eighteenth and nineteenth dynasties. By Mr. Birch they have been supposed to represent the Chaldees. Others have identified them with the Scythians: whilst Bunsen has recognised in the Khita, the Hittites of Scripture, and this last explanation is undoubtedly the true one; for the Sheta of the Assyrian Inscriptions, (written Sveta or sometimes Khetta,) who are certainly the same people as the Khita of the Hieroglyphs, can be distinctly proved from the numerous notices concerning them, to have been the dominant tribe of Palestine, and the ארץ החתים of Joshua, c. i. v. 4, and the מלכי החתים of 2 Kings, c. vii. v. 6, have the same general application. This name חת, indeed, appears to have always been the special and vernacular designation of Palestine, the governors of that province during the period of the Babylonish captivity, taking on their coins the title of מלך רש חת. See the Duc de Luynes's Essay on Phœnicia, p. 76, *sqq.*

city of Tel Barasba. The country beyond the Euphrates[1] he placed under the protection of the god Assarac, the Excellent, while he committed to the god Rimmon, the country between the Euphrates and the Arteri, with its city of Bither[2], which was held by the Sheta. Then I descended into the plains of Elets. The countries of Elets, Shakni, Dayini, Enem (?), Arzaskán, the capital city of Arama, king of Ararat, Lazan and Hubiska, I committed to the charge of Detarasar. Then I went out from the city of Nineveh, and crossing the Euphrates, I attacked and defeated Ahuni, the son of Hateni, in the city of Sitrat, which was situated upon the Euphrates, and which Ahuni had made one of his capitals. The rest of the country I brought under subjection; and Ahuni, the son of Hateni, with his gods and his chief priests, his horses, his sons and his daughters, and all his men of war, I brought away to my country of Assyria. Afterwards I passed through the country of Shelár (or Kelár,) and came to the district of Zoba. I reached the cities belonging to Nikti, and took the city of Yedi, where Nikti dwelt. (A good deal of this part of the inscription I have been obliged to translate almost conjec-

---

[1] The name of the Euphrates is written in Assyrian ⟨cuneiform⟩ or ⟨cuneiform⟩, or optionally with a final *t*, (⟨cuneiform⟩ or ⟨cuneiform⟩ or ⟨cuneiform⟩) and each of these forms must, I think, be sounded *Berát* or *Perat*. The Babylonian orthography was ⟨cuneiform⟩, which, I think, was also pronounced *Huperátah*, although singularly enough this particular term (spelt in many different ways, and generally without the initial sign) was used in all the Assyrian Inscriptions from the earliest period to the latest, as one of the titles of the monarch, and certainly with no reference whatever to the river. For the Babylonian form of the name as it occurs at Behistun, see India-House Inscription, col. vii. l. 45; Bellino's Cylinder, side ii, l. 40; Rich, Pl. IX. No. 4. l. 21; British Museum series, Pl. 18, l. 32; and for the same word written in full, instead of with the syllabic sign ⟨cuneiform⟩ or ⟨cuneiform⟩ or ⟨cuneiform⟩, see British Museum series, Pl. 76, l. 3. Care must be taken not to confound with the name of the Euphrates the word, usually written ⟨cuneiform⟩, and preceded by the determinative of "water," which occurs so often at Khorsabad in connexion with the ⟨cuneiform⟩ or "Chaldees," and in many other places besides; for this term, although pronounced nearly in the same manner as the name of the Euphrates, does in reality apply to the "sea" or "ocean," being perhaps cognate with the Latin *mare*.

[2] Bither is, perhaps, the Biblical פְתוֹר, (Numb. xxii. 5, and Deut. xxiii. 5) but all this part of the Inscription is very difficult, and little dependence can be placed on the translation.

D

turally, for on the Obelisk the confusion is quite bewildering; the engraver having, as I think, omitted a line of the text which he was copying, and the events of the third and fourth year being thus mingled together; while in the Bull Inscription, where the date is preserved, showing that the final action with Ahuni took place in the fourth, and not in the third year, the text is too much mutilated to admit of our obtaining any connected sense. I pass on accordingly to the fifth year.)

"In the fifth year, I went up to the country of Abyari; I took eleven great cities; I besieged Akitta of Erri in his city, and received his tribute.

"In the sixth year, I went out from the city of Nineveh, and proceeded to the country situated on the river Belek[1]. The ruler of the country having resisted my authority, I displaced him and appointed Tsimba to be lord of the district; and I there established the Assyrian sway. I went out from the land on the river Belek, and came to the cities of Tel-Aták (?) and Habaremya. Then I crossed the Upper Euphrates and received tribute from the kings of the Sheta. Afterwards I went out from the land of the Sheta and came to the city of Umen (?) In the city of Umen (?) I raised altars to the great gods. From the city of Umen I went out and came to the city of Barbara. Then Hem-ithra of the country of Atesh[2], and Arhulena

---

[1] The Belek is, I conclude, the Βίλιχος of the Greeks and modern بلخ Bilikh, a large affluent of the Euphrates above the Khabúr.

[2] Atesh is so frequently mentioned in this Inscription, and is apparently a place of so much consequence, as to merit some inquiry into its site. Its connexion with the Sheta would seem to identify it determinately with the Atesh or Ati of the Egyptian records, a city, as Mr. Birch observed in a recent paper, "the ascertaining the site] of which has been deemed one of the greatest desiderata in Egyptian history." (See Trans. of Royal Society of Literature, vol. II. 2nd Ser. p. 336.) Mr. Birch, from an examination of the Egyptian evidence regarding Atesh, came to the conclusion that it was a large city of Syria, to the north of Palestine, and the Cuneiform indications all tend to the same emplacement. That it could not have been far from the sea-coast of Phœnicia, is proved by the Assyrian king having received, whilst sojourning in the land of Atesh, the tribute of Tyre and Sidon, and Byblos; and its uniform association with Hamath would further naturally point out Emessa or Hems, as its modern representative, these two cities having been conjoined in all ages both politically and geographically. It is interesting, therefore, to remark that St. Jerome, in commentating the passage of the Toldoth Beni Noah, where the Zemarite and the Hamathite are spoken of together, explains the former name, which the Jerusalem Targum and all the Oriental Jews identify with Hems or Emessa, as applying to a famous city of Cœlo-Syria, called Edessa. The critics, of course, unanimously suppose that Edessa is here an error for Emessa; but I would inquire if Edessa might not

of Hamath, and the kings of the Sheta, and the tribes which were in alliance with them, arose: setting their forces in battle array they came against me. By the grace of Assarac, the great and powerful god, I fought with them and defeated them; 20,500 of their men I slew in battle, or carried into slavery. Their leaders, their captains, and their men of war, I put in chains.

"In the seventh year, I proceeded to the country belonging to Khabni of Tel-ati. The city of Tel-ati, which was his chief place, and the towns which were dependent on it, I captured and gave up to pillage. I went out from the city of Tel-ati and came to the land watered by the head-streams which form the Tigris. The priests of Assarac in that land raised altars to the immortal gods. I appointed priests to reside in the land to pay adoration to Assarac, the great and powerful god, and to preside over the national worship. The cities of this region which did not acknowledge the god Assarac I brought under subjection, and I here received the tribute of the country of Nahiri.

"In the eighth year, against Sut-Baba, king of Taha-Dunis, appeared Sut-Bel-herat and his followers. The latter led his forces against Sut-Baba and took from him the cities of the land of Beth Takara[1].

have been really an ancient name for Hems, an Hellenic form, indeed, of the Assyrian and Egyptian Atesh. St. Jerome could not possibly have meant the real Edessa, for that city was not in Cœlo-Syria; nor was it ever conjoined with Hamath; nor could the Mesopotamian Edessa possibly represent the Atesh of the Hieroglyphics, for it was not situated upon a river; and the latter feature was the distinguishing local characteristic of the city taken by Sethos I. Whatever may be thought of this attempt to reconcile Atesh with Hems, through St. Jerome's employment of the name of Edessa, it is at any rate certain, that no cities of Syria will so well meet the Cuneiform requirements for Atesh and Hamath, as the modern حمص and حماة, and if we allow for some exaggeration on the part of the Egyptian artists in representing the Orontes as almost equal to the Nile, the pictures of the siege of Atesh, which Mr. Birch conjectures to have given rise to the Greek fable of the Assyrian campaign against Bactria, may, I think, be brought to apply equally well to the same locality of Hems. There are, however, some remarkable ruins on the Orontes above Hems, named قايم الكصل, which are said to be of an Assyrian character, and which may possibly mark the site of Atesh.

[1] I take this name from the Bull Inscriptions, but I do not think the place alluded to can be the famous Chaldean city of Beth Takara, of which mention is so frequently made at Khorsabad. All this part of the Inscription, however, describing the wars of Sut-Baba and Sut-Bel-herat, is exceedingly difficult, and I cannot conjecture even the meaning of several passages.

" In the ninth year, a second time I went up to Armenia[1] and took
the city of Lunanta.   By the assistance of Assarac and Sut, I obtained possession of the person of Sut-Bel-herat.   In the city of Umen
I put him in chains.   Afterwards Sut-Bel-herat, together with his
chief followers, I condemned to slavery.   Then I went down to
Shinar[2], and in the cities of Shinar[3], of Borsippa[4], and of Ketika[5], I

[1] The name here made use of on the Obelisk and in the Inscription on the
Statue from Shergat, (which was dedicated in commemoration of this particular
campaign) is *Hekdi*, and I translate it Armenia, from observing that at Khorsabad, the three names of ⟪cuneiform⟫, ⟪cuneiform⟫, and
⟪cuneiform⟫, or *Hekdi*, *Sheshah*, and *Ararat*, interchange; but I
think that the province of Hekdi must also have included Adiabene; for in the
Shergat Inscription it would certainly seem to intervene between Assyria and
Babylonia.

[2] There is a name here used on the Obelisk and in the Shergat Inscription for
Babylonia which deserves some attention; it is written ⟪cuneiform⟫,
and was pronounced, perhaps, *Pekhodh* or *Pekhods*, being, I think, the same as the
Biblical פקוד, which in Jer. l. 21, and in Ezek. xxiii. 23, is understood to designate some part of the province of Babylon.   The same name is found in several
other inscriptions referring to Babylonia, (see among others, Khors. Ins. p. 152, 12;
ls. 5, 8, 11); and on Bellino's Cylinder it is used almost indifferently for the more
common term ⟪cuneiform⟫.   I take this opportunity, also, of
suggesting that the ארץ מרתים, conjoined with *Pekod* in the verse above
quoted, Jer. l. 21, may be identified with the ⟪cuneiform⟫ of the Inscriptions.
The Cuneiform term is usually in the plural number, as the Hebrew is in the dual;
the two names must be pronounced almost similarly and their geographical application can hardly vary.

[3] I am hardly prepared to maintain that the ancient name of Babylonia,
⟪cuneiform⟫, can be read phonetically as Shinar, though, if
the Biblical title of שנער does anywhere occur in the Inscriptions, this group
of characters has certainly the best claim to be considered its correspondent; for
of the four signs which compose the name, the three last have certainly the powers
n, r, h, and the first may possibly be *s*.   Perhaps it would be a preferable explanation to regard the Cuneiform title as composed entirely of ideographs, and signifying " the country of the god Rah "(?), for the first sign, which has many variants,
seems very frequently to denote a country; the second sign is the determinative of
a god, and was, I think, in the early times used exclusively in that capacity; and
with regard to the third element, we may very well understand that all the various
forms which it takes, and which cannot possibly be brought into phonetic identity,
may be monograms or groups denoting the same deity.   I do not lay much stress

erected altars and founded temples to the great gods. Then I went down to the land of the Chaldees [6], and I occupied their cities, and I

on the particular name Rah, but make use of it as the phonetic value of the characters most commonly employed. The chief objection to this explanation is, that the deity 𒀭 𒂍 is otherwise unknown in Assyrian mythology, (for it would hardly, I suppose, be allowable to compare 'Ρέα or Semiramis, the tutelar divinity of Babylon); but on the other hand, a comparison of a passage in the Khorsabad Inscriptions, Pl. 153, l. 5, where 𒀭 𒀭 𒀭 𒂍 is joined to 𒁹 𒁹 𒂍, with a passage in line 9 of the same plate, where the name of a well-known deity 𒁹 𒀭 𒀭, used geographically, is also joined to the same term, would certainly seem to place 𒀭 𒂍 and 𒀭 𒀭 in the same category of divinity. Of one thing, at any rate, I am pretty well persuaded, that 𒀭 𒁹 𒀭 𒂍 cannot represent Babylon phonetically. The name of Babel, usually written

𒀭 𒌓 𒀭 𒂍 or 𒀭 𒌓 𒀭 𒂍, is never brought, so far as my experience goes, into the remotest alphabetical connexion with the other title, and until therefore I find the one term written with an *r*, 𒀭, instead of an *l*, 𒂍, or the other written with an *l* instead of an *r*, I shall hardly be brought to admit that they can be pronounced in the same manner, or indeed, that they represent phonetically the same name.

[4]. The name of Borsippa, is, I think, undoubted. It occurs in every notice of Babylon from the earliest time to the latest, and the name is written indifferently, Bartsebah, Bartseleh, and Bartsira, another example being thus afforded of the interchange of the *l* or *r* with the *v* or *b*.

[5] The name written 𒂍 𒁹 𒀭 𒂍 on the Obelisk is replaced by 𒁹 𒀭 𒀭 𒂍 in the Bull Inscriptions, but I know nothing of the cities thus indicated, unless they are various forms for the name of Sitace. The chief place of Babylonia, in an Inscription of the Khorsabad period, (British Museum series, Pl. 68, l. 11,) is named 𒀭 𒀭 𒀭 𒀭, and in Pl. 65, l. 19, of the same series, another place is mentioned, which also seems to have been a Babylonian capital, 𒀭 𒀭 𒀭 𒀭 may, perhaps, be the place of which the name is usually written 𒀭 𒀭 𒀭, and which has been already noticed. In a later age, the Jewish Sura was called מתא מחסיא, which somewhat resembles the Cuneiform orthography of 𒀭 𒀭 𒀭.

[6] Although I always translate the Assyrian term 𒀭 𒀭 by Chaldee,

marched on as far even as the tribes who dwelt upon the sea-coast. Afterwards in the city of Shinar, I received the tribute of the kings of the Chaldees, Hateni, the son of Dákri, and Baga-Sut, the son of Hukni, gold, silver, gems and pearls.

"In the tenth year, for the eighth time I crossed the Euphrates. I took the cities belonging to Ara-lura[1] of the town of Shalumas[2], and gave them up to pillage. Then I went out from the cities of Shalumas, and I proceeded to the country belonging to Arama, (who was king of Ararat.) I took the city of Arnia, which was the capital of the country, and I gave up to pillage one hundred of the dependent towns. I slew the wicked, and I carried off the treasures.

"At this time Hem-ithra, king of Atesh, and Arhulena, king of

from the location of the tribe to which the title belongs in Lower Chaldæa, that is, between Babylonia Proper and the sea, I am by no means sure that the Cuneiform characters will represent that name phonetically; nor am I satisfied that the Greek term Χαλδαῖα, for the Biblical בַּשְׂדִּי, is of itself a genuine ancient form. At the same time, as the character ⟦cuneiform⟧ has properly the full syllabic power of *l-v*, it may, according to my system, represent one of those sounds without the other, and may even admit an initial vowel, or, which is the same thing in Babylonian, an aspiration; so that I think it quite possible ⟦cuneiform⟧ ⟦cuneiform⟧ and ⟦cuneiform⟧ ⟦cuneiform⟧ may be read *Halah* and *Haldi*, for Calah and Chaldi. Other readings have occurred to me for ⟦cuneiform⟧ ⟦cuneiform⟧, such as *Labdi* for Nabti, "the Nabathæans;" or *Ludi*, the Lud of Scripture, joined with Persia and Phut, (which latter is certainly the *Putiyá* of the Nakhsh-i-Rustam Inscription) in Ezek. c. 27, v. 10, and perhaps the Luten or Ruten of the Hieroglyphs; but on geographical as well as etymological considerations I prefer adhering to my translation of "*Chaldee.*"

[1] This name is written indifferently ⟦cuneiform⟧ ⟦cuneiform⟧ ⟦cuneiform⟧ and ⟦cuneiform⟧ ⟦cuneiform⟧ ⟦cuneiform⟧ ⟦cuneiform⟧, leading to the inference that the monogram ⟦cuneiform⟧ denotes the same god as the group ⟦cuneiform⟧ ⟦cuneiform⟧, but I have not otherwise met with either of these forms in connexion with the Assyrian Pantheon.

[2] The city, of which the name is written ⟦cuneiform⟧ ⟦cuneiform⟧ ⟦cuneiform⟧ or ⟦cuneiform⟧ ⟦cuneiform⟧ ⟦cuneiform⟧ ⟦cuneiform⟧, and which was the capital of the Hittites, and the chief place apparently in Syria, must represent, it would seem, either Baalbek, or Damascus, or Jerusalem; but I have not yet been able to satisfy myself to which place the notices in the Inscriptions are most applicable, nor, owing to the strangely contradictory employment of the character ⟦cuneiform⟧, can I determine with any certainty the true form of the name.

Hamath, and the twelve kings of the tribes who were in alliance with them[1], came forth arraying their forces against me. They met me, and we fought a battle in which I defeated them, making prisoners of their leaders, and their captains, and their men of war, and putting them in chains.

"In the eleventh year, I went out from the city of Nineveh, and for the ninth time crossed the Euphrates. I took the eighty-seven cities belonging to Ara-lura, and one hundred cities belonging to Arama, and I gave them up to pillage. I settled the country of Khamána, and passing by the country of Yeri, I went down to the cities of Hamath, and took the city of Esdimak, and eighty-nine of the dependent towns, slaying the wicked ones and carrying off the treasures. Again, Hem-ithra, king of Atesh, Arhulena, king of Hamath, and the twelve kings of the tribes, (or in one copy, the twelve kings of the Sheta) who were in alliance with them, came forth, levying war upon me; they arrayed their forces against me. I fought with them and defeated them, slaying 10,000 of their men, and carrying into slavery their captains, and leaders, and men of war. Afterwards I went up to the city of Habbaril, one of the chief cities belonging to Arama (of Ararat,) and there I received the tribute of Berbaranda, the king of Shetina, gold, silver, horses, sheep and oxen, &c., &c.[2] I then went up to the country of Khamána, where I founded palaces and cities.

"In the twelfth year, I marched forth from Nineveh, and for the tenth time I crossed the Euphrates, and went up to the city of Sevarra-

---

[1] I have sometimes thought that the twelve tribes who are confounded with the Hittites, and who confederate with the kings of Atesh and Hamath against the Assyrians, might represent the children of Israel, but such an identification can be at present but a mere conjecture. In one passage they are spoken of, I think, as "the twelve tribes of the Upper and Lower country;" (the word that I translate " Upper " being the epithet applied to the Upper Zab, which is crossed on the march from Nineveh to Media ;) and if accordingly the Jews should be the people indicated, the notice must be supposed to refer to them soon after their arrival in Palestine, from "the Upper and Lower country" of Egypt, a somewhat greater antiquity being thus given to the Inscriptions of Nimrud than I should be otherwise disposed to claim for them.

[2] This tribute is represented in the fifth row of sculptures upon the Obelisk. Perhaps the true reading of the name of the tribe is the Sevtina or Sebtina, for as the letter ⸕ represents the *s* and *b* indifferently, the inference is that it must have originally possessed the full syllabic power of *Seb*. I conjecture the Sevtina, who are very frequently spoken of in the early Assyrian Inscriptions, but rarely or ever in the later, to be the Shairutena of the Hieroglyphs. They inhabited some parts of Syria, but I have no clue to their particular emplacement.

huben. I slew the wicked and carried off the treasures from thence to my own country.

"In the thirteenth year, I descended to the plains dependent on the city of Assar-animet. I went to the district of Yáta. I took the forts of the country of Yáta, slaying the evil-disposed and carrying off all the wealth of the country.

"In the fourteenth year, I raised the country and assembled a great army; with 120,000 warriors I crossed the Euphrates. Then it came to pass, that Hem-ithra, king of Atesh, and Arhulena, king of Hamath, and the twelve kings of the tribes of the upper and lower country, collected their forces together, and came before me offering battle. I engaged with them and defeated them; their leaders, and captains, and men of war I cast into chains.

"In the fifteenth year, I went to the country of Nahiri, and established my authority throughout the country about the head streams which form the Tigris. In the district of Akhábi I celebrated (some great religious ceremony, probably, which is obscurely described, and which I am quite unable to render).

"Afterwards I descended to the plains of Lanbuna, and devastated the cities of Arama, king of Ararat[1], and all the country about the head waters of the Euphrates; and I abode in the country about the rivers which form the Euphrates, and there I set up altars to the supreme gods, and left priests in the land to superintend the worship. Hasá, king of Dayini[2], there paid me his homage and brought in his tribute of horses, and I established the authority of my empire throughout the land dependent on his city.

"In the sixteenth year, I crossed the river Zab, and went against the country of the Arians[3]. Sut-mesitek, the king of the Arians, I put

[1] I may here notice, once for all, that there is no doubt whatever about the reading of Ararat, nor its identity with Armenia; for both at Nakhsh-i-Rustam and Behistun, the Persian Armina is represented in the Babylonian translation by Hararat, written nearly in the same manner as at Khorsabad. I have added this note as the sheets are passing through the press, in consequence of remarking that Dr. Hincks has mistaken the name of Ararat for that of Chorasmia.

[2] I conjecture the Dayini or Dayani to be the Tahia of the Hieroglyphs, Scriptural דיהא, and Δάοι of Herodotus, Lib. i. c. 125.

[3] The identification of the ►]][⟨⟨ ►]]]] with the Arians (or Άριοι, whom Herodotus mentions as the ancient inhabitants of Media, Lib. vii. c. 62) is very doubtful. The people mentioned in the Inscriptions, however, evidently dwelt within the mountain range east of Assyria, and were neighbours of the Medes. The name seems to have been become obsolete at the Khorsabad period of history.

in chains, and I brought his wives, and his warriors, and his gods, captives to my country of Assyria; and I appointed Yanvu, the son of Khanab, to be king over the country in his place.

"In the seventeenth year, I crossed the Euphrates and went up to the country of Khamána, where I founded palaces and cities.

"In the eighteenth year, for the sixteenth time I crossed the Euphrates. Khazakan of Atesh came forth to fight; 1121 of his captains, and 460 of his superior chiefs, with the troops they commanded, I defeated in this war.

[It was to commemorate this campaign, that the Colossal Bulls found in the centre of the Mound at Nimrud, were set up. The inscription upon them recording the wars, is of course far more detailed than the brief summary on the Obelisk, and I may as well therefore give my reading of it.

It commences with a geographical catalogue. "The upper and lower countries of Nahiri, the extensive land which worshipped the god Husi, Khamáua and the Sheta, the countries along the course of the Tigris, and the countries watered by the Euphrates, from Belats to Shakni, from Shakni to Meluda, from Meluda to Dayáni, from Dayáni to Arzeskán, from Arzeskán to Latsán, from Latsán to Hubiska; the Arians and the tribes of the Chaldees who dwell upon the sea-coast.

"In the eighteenth year, for the sixteenth time I crossed the Euphrates. Then Khazakan of Atesh collected his warriors and came forth; these warriors he committed to a man of Aranersa, who had administered the country of Lemnan. Him he appointed chief of his army. I engaged with him and defeated him, slaying and carrying into slavery 13,000 of his fighting men, and making prisoners 1121 of his captains, and 460 superior officers, with their cohorts."

I now return to the Obelisk.]

"In the nineteenth year, for the eighteenth time I crossed the Euphrates. I went up again to Khamána, and founded more palaces and temples.

"In the twentieth year, for the twentieth time I crossed the Euphrates. I went up to the country of Beráhui. I took the cities, and despoiled them of their treasures.

"In the twenty-first year, for the twentieth time I crossed the Euphrates, and again went up to the country of Khazakan of Atesh. I occupied his territory, and while there received tribute from the countries of Tyre, of Sidon, and of Gubal[1].

---

[1] Gubal is the Greek Βύβλος. The form of גְבַל occurs in several passages of Scripture, (see Ezek. xxvii. 9, and 1 Kings v. 32); and the same orthography

"In the twenty-second year, for the twenty-first time I crossed the Euphrates and marched to the country of Tubal[1]. Then I received the submission of the twenty-four kings of Tubal, and I went on to the country of Atta, to the gold country, to Belui, and to Ta-Esferem[2].

"In the twenty-third year, I again crossed the Euphrates and occupied the city of Huidara, the strong-hold of Ellal of Meluda; and the kings of Tubal again came in to me and I received their tribute.

"In the twenty-fourth year, I crossed the river Zab, and passing away from the land of Kharkhar[3], went up to the country of the Arians. Yanvu, whom I had made king of the Arians, had thrown off his allegiance, so I put him in chains. I captured the city of Esaksha and took Beth Telabon, Beth Everek, and Beth Tsida, his principal cities. I slew the evil-disposed, and plundered the treasures, and gave the cities over to pillage. I then went out from the land of the Arians, and received the tribute of the twenty-seven kings of the Persians. Afterwards I removed from the land of the Persians and entered the territory of the Medes, going on to Ratsir and Kharkhar; I occupied the several cities of Kákhidra, of Tarzánem, of Irleban, of Akhirablud, and the towns which depended on them. I punished the evil-disposed. I confiscated the treasures and gave the cities over to

was retained until a late period upon the coins of the city. See the Duc de Luynes's Essay, "Sur la Numismatique de la Phœnicie," p. 88, *sqq.*

[1] The Syrian tribe of Tubal, connected, in all probability, if not identical with the תובל or תבל of Scripture, will be more particularly noticed in my remarks on the Khorsabad Inscriptions.

[2] I have ventured to read 𒀭𒁹 𒂊 𒐊 𒂊𒁹 phonetically, as it here certainly represents the name of a country; but the term, which is of very common occurrence, usually denotes some well-known natural object, (perhaps a palm-tree,) and the initial character is determinative. The same word, I may add, is used to designate a city of Babylon in the E. I. H. Insc., col. iv. l. 27.

[3] The land of Kharkhar, which is very frequently mentioned in the Inscriptions of Nimrud, of Khorsabad, and of Van, was certainly a part of Armenia. There are two people known in Armenian history whose names nearly resemble the Cuneiform title, the Karkarians (Γαργαρεῖς of Strabo), and the Khorkhorunians, descended from Khorh, son of Haig. The latter, however, who dwelt upon the lake Van, and were of much traditional celebrity, have certainly the best claim to be identified with the Cuneiform Kharkhar (see St. Martin's Armenia, vol. II. p. 246). The siege of the city of Kharkhar, capital of the province, is represented in the Khorsabad sculptures, Salle II. No. 7; and this may possibly be the same place as the modern city of Van, for the hill on which the castle is built retains the name of Khorkhor to the present day: though as the Kharkhar, which is mentioned in the Inscriptions on the Van rock, appears to be a foreign place, the mere coincidence of name is by no means sufficient to prove an identity.

pillage, and I established the authority of my empire in the city of Kharkhar. Yanvu, the son of Khaban (usually written Khanab), with his wives and his gods, and his sons and daughters, his servants and all his property, I carried away captive into my country of Assyria[1].

"In the twenty-fifth year, I crossed the Euphrates and received the tribute of the kings of the Sheta. I passed by the country of Khamána and came to the cities of Akti of Berhui. The city of Tabura, his strong-hold, I took by assault. I slew those who resisted and plundered the treasures; and all the cities of the country I gave over to pillage. Afterwards in the city of Bahura, the capital city of Aram, son of Hagus, I dedicated a temple to the god Rimmon, and I also built a royal palace in the same place.

"In the twenty-sixth year, for the seventh time I passed through the country of Khamána. I went on to the cities of Akti of Berhui, and I inhabited the city of Tanaken, which was the strong-hold of Etlak; there I performed the rites which belong to the worship of Assarac, the supreme god; and I received as tribute from the country, gold and silver, and corn, and sheep, and oxen. Then I went out from the city of Tanaken, and I came to the country of Leman. The people resisted me, but I subdued the country by force. I took the cities and slew their defenders; and the wealth of the people, with their cattle and corn and moveables, I sent as booty to my country of Assyria. I gave all their cities over to pillage. Then I went on to the country of Methets, where the people paid their homage, and I received gold and silver as their tribute. I appointed Akharriyadon,

[1] I infer, from the geographical distribution contained in this paragraph, that the Persian tribes, when they were thus first brought in contact with the Assyrians, had not yet turned to the southward in their immigration from beyond the Oxus, or, at any rate, had not yet reached Persia Proper. The  or Arians, who were first met with after the passage of the Zab, inhabited probably Central Media. The Persian tribes I should place about Rhages and the Caspian Straits (the date of the Nimrud Inscriptions being thus apparently synchronous with the composition of the first Fargard of the Vendidad). The Medes might then be understood as the inhabitants of Atropatene, and Kharkhar would be Pers-armenia. I do not of course give these emplacements as certain, but it would be difficult, according to any other explanation, to bring the tribes and countries indicated into geographical relation. I may add that it is, I think, undoubtedly in allusion to the Kharkhar of the Inscriptions, that Alexander Polyhistor, quoting Berosus, says of the ark or vessel in which Xisuthrus escaped from the flood, ἔτι μέρος τι ἐν τοῖς Κορκυραίων ὄρεσι τῆς Ἀρμενίας διαμένειν. Syncell. Chron. 28; Eus. Chron. 5. 8.

the son of Akti, to be king over them. Afterwards I went up to Khamána, where I founded more palaces and temples; until at length I returned to my country of Assyria.

"In the twenty-seventh year, I assembled the captains of my army, and I sent Detarasar of Ittána, the general of the forces, in command of my warriors to Armenia; he proceeded to the land of Khamána, and in the plains belonging to the city of Ambaret, he crossed the river Artseni[1]. Asiduri of Armenia, hearing of the invasion, collected his cohorts and came forth against my troops, offering them battle; my forces engaged with him and defeated him, and the country at once submitted to my authority.

"In the twenty-eighth year, whilst I was residing in the city of Calah, a revolt took place on the part of the tribes of the Shetina. They were led on by Sherrila, who had succeeded to the throne on the death of Labarni, the former king. Then I ordered the general of my army, Detarasar of Ittána, to march with my cohorts and all my troops against the rebels. Detarasar accordingly crossed the Upper Euphrates, and marching into the country established himself in the capital city, Kanalá. Then Sherrila, who was seated on the throne, by the help of the great god Assarac, I obtained possession of his person, and his officers, and the chiefs of the tribes of the Shetina who had thrown off their allegiance and revolted against me, together with the sons of Sharila, and the men who administered affairs, and imprisoned or punished all of them; and I appointed Ar-hasit of Sirzakisba to be king over the entire land. I exacted a great tribute also from the land, consisting of gold and silver and precious stones, and ebony, &c., &c., &c.; and I established the national worship throughout the land, making a great sacrifice in the capital city of Kanalá, in the temple which had been there raised to the gods.

"In the twenty-ninth year, I assembled my warriors and captains, and I ascended with them to the country of the Lek. I ac-

---

[1] If the name here written 𒀭 𒂍 𒀭 𒈨 be really Khamána (and as the 𒀭 and 𒈨 commonly interchange, I can hardly doubt the identity), we must give a somewhat greater extension to the country indicated than I have before proposed. We must consider Khamána, indeed, not only to apply to the true 'Αμάνος, but to include a part of Taurus; for the river Artseni, crossed on the march from Assyria to Ararat, or "the Great Armenia," can only be the 'Αρσένιας of the Greeks (modern ارسيان); and Ambaret, or perhaps Akberet, I should suppose to be the Armenian Kharbert, or, as it is usually called, Kharpoot.

cepted the homage of the cities of the land, and I then went on to Shenába.

"In the thirtieth year, whilst I was still residing in the city of Calah, I summoned Detarasar, the general of my army, and I sent him forth to war in command of my cohorts and forces. He crossed the river Zab, and first came to the cities of Hubiska; he received the tribute of Daten of Hubiska; and he went out from thence and came to the country belonging to Mekadul of Melakari, where tribute was duly paid. Leaving the cities of Melakari, he then went on to the country of Huelka of Minni. Huelka of Minni had thrown off his allegiance and declared himself independent, establishing his seat of government in the city of Tsiharta. My general therefore put him in chains, and carried off his flocks and herds and all his property, and gave his cities over to pillage. Passing out from the country of Minni he next came to the territory of Selshen of Kharta; he took possession of the city of Maharsar, the capital of the country, and of all the towns which depended on it; and Selshen and his sons he made prisoners and sent to his country, despatching to me their tribute of horses, male and female. He then went into the country of Sardera, and received the tribute of Artaheri of Sardera; he afterwards marched to Persia and obtained the tribute of the kings of the Persians; and he captured many more cities between Persia and Assyria, and he brought all their riches and treasures with him to Assyria.

"In the thirty-first year, a second time, whilst I abode in the city of Calah, occupied in the worship of the gods Assarac, Hem, and Nebo, I summoned the general of my army, Detarasar of Ittána, and I sent him forth to war in command of my troops and cohorts. He went out accordingly, in the first place, to the territories of Daten of Hubiska, and received his tribute; then he proceeded to Enseri, the capital city of the country of Bazatsera, and he occupied the city of Anseri, and the thirty-six other towns of the country of Bazatsera; he continued his march to the land of Armenia, and he gave over to pillage fifty cities belonging to that territory. He afterwards proceeded to Ladsán, and received the tribute of Hubu of Ladsán, and of the districts of Minni, of Bariana, of Kharran, of Sharrum, of Andi, (and another district of which the name is lost), sheep, oxen, and horses, male and female. Afterwards he went on to a district (of which the name is lost), and he gave up to pillage the cities Biaria and Sitihuria, cities of consideration, together with the twenty-two towns which were attached to them. And he afterwards penetrated as far as the land of the Persians, taking possession of the cities of

Baiset, Shel Khamána, and Akori-Khamána, all of them places of strength, and of the twenty-three towns which depended on them; he slew those who resisted, and he carried off the wealth of the cities. And he afterwards moved to the country of the Arians, where by the help of the gods Assarac and Sut, he captured their cities and continued his march to the country of Kharets, taking and despoiling 250 towns; until at length he descended into the plains of Esmes, above the country of Umen[1]."

(It is extremely difficult to distinguish throughout these last two paragraphs between the 1st and 3rd persons. In fact, the grammatical prefixes which mark the persons are frequently put one for the other even in the same sentence. From the opening clause of the para-

---

[1] I will not pretend at present to discuss the geography of either of these two last campaigns; for though many of the names, such as Hubiska, Bazatsera, otherwise Mekhatseri, Ladsán, &c., are well known in the Inscriptions, I have not been able to discover anything certain with regard to their positions, further than that they were contiguous to Northern Media and Armenia. The province of Minni, however, which is mentioned in the campaign of the thirtieth year, and which occupies a conspicuous place in the Inscriptions both of Khorsabad and Van (the name being written indifferently as ⟨⟨ ⊢⊣Y YY YY and ⋿Y ⊢⊢Y ⊢⊣Y YY YY) is certainly the מִנִּי of Scripture, associated by Jeremiah (c. li. v. 27) with Ararat and Ashchenaz, and also spoken of by Nicolaus of Damascus under the form of Μινυάς. I may also hazard a conjecture that the אַשְׁכְּנַז Ashkenaz of Scripture is the Arzeskan of the Inscriptions, which was the capital city of Arama, king of Ararat, the two names being almost identical, if we admit a metathesis in the orthography. Ashkenaz must at any rate necessarily have some Cuneiform correspondent, and I know of no name but Arzeskan that at all resembles it. The similarity of the Arama YY ⋿⊤⊢Y Y⊢ of the Inscriptions with the Armenian king Aram, sixth in descent from Haig, cannot of course be overlooked; but I would hardly propose to draw any historical inference from this coincidence of name. I will only add that the notice of the Persians in both of these campaigns, in evident connection with tribes and countries belonging to Northern Media and Armenia, is to my mind strongly confirmatory of the supposition that at the date of the Nimrud Inscriptions the tribes in question were still encamped at the foot of the mountains south of the Caspian, in those seats which the traditions of the race identified with the exploits of Feridoun and his successors. I believe indeed that these Cuneiform notices of the Persians will go far to verify the suspicion which has been long entertained, of the subjection of the race to the Assyrian yoke being figured under the tyrannical rule of the usurper Zohák, and will enable us in the end to introduce something like chronological accuracy and order into the myths and traditions embodied in the Shah-námeh.

graphs, I certainly understand that the Assyrian general conducted both of these expeditions into High Asia; yet, it would seem as if the king in chronicling the war, wished to appropriate the achievements to himself.)

It remains that I should notice the Epigraphs which are engraved on the Obelisk above the five series of figures. These epigraphs contain a sort of register of the tribute sent in by five different nations to the Assyrian king; but they do not follow the series of offerings as they are represented in the sculpture with any approach to exactitude.

The first epigraph records the receipt of the tribute from Shehuá of Ladsán, a country which joined Armenia, and which I presume, therefore, to be connected with the Lazi and Lazistán.

The second line of offerings are said to have been sent by Yahua, son of Hubiri, a prince of whom there is no mention in the annals, and of whose native country therefore I am ignorant.

This is followed by the tribute of a country which is called Misr, and which there are good grounds for supposing to be Egypt, inasmuch as we are sure from the numerous indications afforded to the position in the Inscriptions of Khorsabad, that Misr adjoined Syria, and as the same name, (that is, a name pronounced in the same manner, though written with different phonetic characters,) is given at Behistun as the Babylonian equivalent of the Persian Mudráya[1]. Misr is not once mentioned in the Obelisk annals, and it may be presumed, therefore, to have remained in complete subjection to Assyria during the whole of Temen-bar's reign.

The fourth tribute is that of Sut-pal-adan, of the country of Shekhi, probably a Babylonian or Elymæan prince, who is not otherwise mentioned; and the series is closed by the tribute of Barberanda,

---

[1] The Misr of Behistun and Nakhsh-i-Rustam, answering to *Mudráya*, is written 𒈹 𒈹, whilst the name occurs under a variety of forms in the Inscriptions of Assyria, the first character being ➤⟨, ➤⟨⟨ or ⟨⟨⟨, equal to *m* or *v*; the second, ⟨⟩ ⟨⟩, or ⟨⟩ equal to *s*; and the third, uniformly ➤⟨⟨⟨ or *r*. There can be little doubt therefore, I think, about the identity of the names; and the geographical indications of the Khorsabad Inscriptions are applicable to Egypt, and to Egypt only. As the name of מצר, by which the Jews designated Egypt, was unknown in the country itself, it is highly interesting to find that it was in use amongst the Assyrians, at as early a period as the Nimrud sculptures.

the Shetina, a Syrian tribe, which I rather think is the same as the Sharutana of the hieroglyphic writing.

I cannot pretend, at present, to identify the various articles which are named in these epigraphs; gold and silver, pearls and gems, ebony and ivory, may be made out, I think, with more or less certainty; but I cannot conjecture the nature of many other of the offerings; they may be rare woods, or aromatic gums, or metals, or even such articles as glass or porcelain.

With regard to the animals, those alone which I can certainly identify are horses and camels, the latter being, I think, described as " beasts of the desert with the double back[1]."

I do not think any of the remarkable animals, such as the elephant, the wild bull, the unicorn, the antelope, and the monkeys and baboons, are specified in the epigraphs; but it is possible they may be spoken of as rare animals from the river of Arki and the country beyond the sea.

I have now finished my general sketch of the Obelisk Inscription. There are several fragments attaching to bas-reliefs in the centre palace of Nimrud, which probably record further exploits of Temenbar's reign,—but I have not yet met with the king's name upon any of them; and the expeditions of all the Assyrian kings were so very similar, not only in the countries attacked, and in the conduct of the campaigns, but even in respect to the phraseology employed to describe the wars, that without the direct proof of identity afforded by proper

---

[1] Dr. Hincks has declared this explanation to be quite untenable, and I am not prepared myself to support it very warmly. As the term 𒀭 𒌍 𒀸, however, denotes ordinarily some natural feature, whilst preceded by the determinative 𒄑, it represents "a camel," it is certainly most reasonable to explain the connexion between the two meanings by supposing the camel to be the beast especially belonging to that natural feature; and if this be admitted, "desert" will assuredly be a more suitable reading for 𒀭 𒌍 𒀸 than "forest." There would be no impropriety also in connecting the desert with Lebanon, especially where, as in line 8 of the Nimrud Standard Inscription, a great territorial boundary is indicated, for a phrase of very similar structure and application occurs in the fourth verse of the first chapter of Joshua :—" From the wilderness and this Lebanon, even unto the great river, the river Euphrates." At the same time I fully admit the force of Dr. Hincks's observations, which I have just read in page 68 of his Paper on the Khorsabad Inscriptions; and I bear a most willing testimony to the great sagacity which he has brought to bear on this and many other points connected with the Cuneiform Inscriptions, and which very frequently has rendered him independent of data.

names, it is never safe to assume the king to whom the annals may belong.

Of the son and grandson of Temen-bar II., little is known beside the names; the name of the one is compounded of the titles of the two gods, Husi or Shemir, and Hem; and thus, although generally written Husi-hem, it may also read Shemir-hem, which certainly sounds very like the Greek Semiramis. The other is named Hevenk, like the grandfather of Sardanapalus, and it is to this king, Hevenk (or Evechius) II., that we are indebted for the genealogical tree which carries up the ancestry of the family, at any rate to Temen-bar I., and which contains a passage that may possibly name Beltakat, the twentieth in ascent, who first instituted the Assyrian monarchy[1].

With Hevenk II. terminates the series of kings immediately connected with Sardanapalus. Owing to domestic troubles or to foreign invasion, there appears after this king to have been an interruption of the royal line; and in the interval which elapsed before the succession was restored, a very considerable change may be shown to have taken place in the manners and customs of the inhabitants of the country. So complete, indeed, does the social revolution appear to Mr. Layard, that he conjectures a new race to have peopled the country, or at any rate, a new dynasty with a new religion to have acquired the kingdom. On this point, however, I am not altogether of Mr. Layard's opinion. I am willing to admit an interregnum; and I think it even probable, as the king who restored the empire is entirely silent on the subject of his genealogy, that he was not a member of the old imperial family in the line of direct descent; but at the same time, I feel pretty certain, that no very long period of time could have elapsed between Evechius II. and the builder of Khorsabad. The titles employed by the latter, although unused by Sardanapalus, are to be found in the genealogical inscription of Hevenk II.[2]; the language, also, of the inscriptions of Nimrud and Khorsabad is absolutely identical; not only, too, were the same gods worshipped by the restored as by the old dynasty, but the gods were grouped in the same combinations[3];

[1] See British Museum series, Pl. 70, l. 25. There is no certain genealogy in this Inscription above Temen-bar II., for although four other royal names are mentioned, it is extremely doubtful how they may be connected.

[2] I refer to the title "king of Sabiri and Sheshak," which is found line 21 of the Inscription in question, applied to Katibar, who was also king of Assyria.

[3] I observe, however, that the worship of Ashteroth ( or , *Ashtera*,) seems to have been introduced into Assyria during this interval; for the name, although of very frequent occurrence in the

and furthermore, we have evidence that the Khorsabad king actually
inhabited the north-west Palace of Nimrud, two of his inscriptions
having been found there which record how he repaired the great
palace of Halah, originally built by Sardanapalus, "who (as I doubtfully read the legend) was the fourth in ascent from me[1]."

If this reading should in the sequel prove to be correct, all uncer-
tainty with regard to the relative chronology will be removed, for
Hevenk II., Husi-hem, and Temen-bar II., will exactly fill up the
interval indicated between the Khorsabad king and Sardanapalus, and
it will thus be shown that notwithstanding the interregnum, the line
was considered to have been kept on in a continuous succession.

I have particularly noticed this apparent connexion of the two
dynasties, as the impression appears to be pretty general, that whatever may be the antiquity allowed to the Nimrud series of kings, the
line commencing with the builder of Khorsabad must at any rate
represent what is usually termed the lower dynasty of Assyria, that is,
the monarchs mentioned in Scripture, who were contemporary with
the kings of Israel and Judah.   Now in a question of this sort, with
the limited and intractable materials that are alone available to our
research, certainty is impossible.   Positiveness must of itself create
suspicion, for it is a proof that the subject cannot have been thoroughly
investigated.   I would not pretend for my own part to pronounce
authoritatively, that the kings of the lower or restored dynasty of
Assyria were, or were not, the royal line mentioned in Scripture.   My
opinion at present is, I confess, against the identification, but the
evidence is pretty nearly balanced, and if the great difficulty, the
dissimilarity of names, were removed, I might possibly become a
convert to the belief that in the three kings, who built the Palace of

Inscriptions of Khorsabad, is never once met with in the earlier annals of Nimrud.
The term Ashtera, however, is often used simply for a goddess, as in the
phrase, "the gods and goddesses inhabiting Assyria." See Khorsabad Plates,
No. 131, ls. 8 and 20, &c.

[1] See British Museum series, Pl. 33, l. 13. As the characters ►‍𐎠 and
►‍𐎠 interchange in the name of the Euphrates, and as the former is often used
after a king's name, apparently as a title or epithet, I believe I must abandon the
idea of their representing "third" and "fourth" in the two passages where they refer
respectively to Temen-bar I. and Sardanapalus.   That 𐎠 𐎠 𐎠 𐎠 𐎠
however signifies "an ancestor" or "one going before," I consider to be almost
certain, not only from a very similar expression at Behistun, but from the occurrence of the phrase in several Inscriptions at Khorsabad, where the context proves
the sense; compare amongst others, line 8 of Pl. 153, and see British Museum
series, Pl. 76, ls. 22 and 23.

Khorsabad, who founded Mespila, and who constructed the lions in the south-west Palace of Nimrud, we had the Biblical Shalmaneser, Sennacherib, and Esarhaddon.

This subject is of so much interest, that before running over the general contents of the inscriptions of the different kings, I will give the heads of the argument both for and against the identification.

Firstly then with regard to Shalmaneser: the Sargon of Isaiah, who sent his general, Tartan, against Ashdod, at the commencement apparently of the reign of Hoshea, king of Israel, is almost certainly the same king who is usually named Shalmaneser[1]; it may be supposed, therefore, that the king bore these two names indifferently. Now I do not think that the Assyrian name of the Khorsabad king will read phonetically, either Sargon or Shalmaneser, but it may be made to assimilate with the former name, inasmuch as the first element of it denotes " a king," to which amongst other words, *Sar* answers in Chaldee[2]; and the second element, which reads *tsin* or *du*, interchanges in other names with *kon*[3], leading to the inference that

---

[1] Compare Isaiah xx. 1 with 2 Kings xviii. 17.

[2] The first element of the name is ⟦cuneiform⟧ (which is the Assyrian form of the Babylonian ⟦cuneiform⟧) or ⟨⟨, these characters being abbreviations or monograms for the word "king." I have already mentioned that the word of which ⟦cuneiform⟧ is the abbreviation, is written at Behistun at full length as *arkau* or *arko;* but I am in great doubt whether ⟨⟨ should be made to assimilate with this title, or whether it may not stand for Melik. The word שׁר properly signifies merely " a prince," but as the root שׁרר has the general sense of " ruling " or "having dominion," we may reasonably suppose a derivative from it to be applied to "a king" or "supreme ruler."

[3] It is with some doubt that I render the term ⟦cuneiform⟧ by *tsin*. This reading, indeed, depends on the character ⟦cuneiform⟧ being the same as ⟦cuneiform⟧ or ⟦cuneiform⟧, and although the one form is certainly often interchanged with the other, I am by no means assured of their identity. For an instance of the interchange of ⟦cuneiform⟧ with ⟦cuneiform⟧ see the name of the Chaldæan king at Khorsabad, which occurring as it does in almost every inscription, is written indifferently ⟦cuneiform⟧ and ⟦cuneiform⟧. It has sometimes occurred to me that the Khorsabad king's name is to be found in the Ἀνακυνδαραξης of the Greeks. ⟦cuneiform⟧, might very well be made to read Ἀνακυν, and δαραξης greatly resembles ⟦Zend⟧, *drukhs*, although the union of Assyrian and Zend is somewhat incongruous.

E 2

tsin, du, and *kon,* were synonyms, which might be optionally employed.   As a further argument, also, that the popular name of the
Khorsabad king was really Sargon, I must repeat the observation
which I have already made in treating of the nomenclature of the
ruins; namely, that the city excavated by M. Botta is stated in the
inscriptions to have borne the same name as its founder[1], and that as
late as the Arab conquest the site of Khorsabad actually retained in
the country, the old Syrian title of Sarghun.

  This similarity of name, however, is perhaps the least striking of
the coincidences between the Khorsabad king and the Shalmaneser of
history.   Shalmaneser we know attacked Hoshea, because he was in
communication with Sabaco, king of Egypt.   The king of Egypt
mentioned in the Khorsabad Inscriptions, dating perhaps five years
earlier, is Biarka or Biarku, a title which somewhat resembles that of
Bocchoris, the king whom Sabaco dethroned.   We further learn from
Josephus, quoting from Menander, that Shalmaneser sent a force to
Cyprus to assist the islanders against Tyre[2]; and it is thus highly
interesting to find that an inscription which has lately been discovered
in the island of Cyprus, and which appears to commemorate the libe-
ration of the islanders, belongs to the king of Assyria, who is known
as the builder of Khorsabad[3].   An expedition against Ashdod is
described at Khorsabad, which may very well be that noticed in
Isaiah, and the king always names Ashdod among his tributary cities,
whilst Tyre and Sidon are excluded from the list, in accordance
apparently with the testimony of Menander, that Tyre successfully
resisted Shalmaneser's five years' siege.   Among the countries overrun
by the Khorsabad king we also find in one inscription the name of
Yehuda[4], in connexion with that of Hamath, and although without
further evidence I would not venture for my own part to identify the
geographical position, I can well understand that a sanguine inter-

[1] That is, it is the name of the king, preceded by a noun of locality. This
noun is written ⟨⟨⟩⟩, and from its interchanging with ⊐◁⊐|,
(see British Museum series, Pl. 44, 18th variant,) it may be conjectured to have
the phonetic value of *amen.* In use, however, it is equivalent to the Beth, Tel,
Hazar, Kefer, Kiriath, &c., used in Arabic and Hebrew geography.

[2] See Cory's Fragments, p. 199.

[3] I examined this Inscription a short time back in the Museum at Berlin, and
I have since received a very perfect paper cast of it, through the kindness of
Dr. Olfers. It is very similar to the Standard Inscription of Khorsabad, but
contains a brief local notice of much interest.

[4] See British Museum series, No. 33, 1. 8.   The name is written
𒂍𒅀 𒐍 𒅀.

preter would be disposed to fasten on the passage as a notice of the conquest of Samaria.

I now go on to the next king, the builder of the great palace of Koyunjik, and the son of the king at Khorsabad, whose actions, it must be admitted, have a good deal of resemblance to those of Sargon or Shalmaneser. Of course if the father be Shalmaneser the son will be Sennacherib, and it has been lately stated by a scholar, Dr. Hincks, who has made considerable progress in decyphering the Assyrian inscriptions, that the Cuneiform orthography actually gives that name. I cannot, however, I confess, persuade myself of the possibility of such a reading. In some of the many forms which the name takes the two last letters are *r* and *m*, and the initial monogram may have the power of *s*, but there is no other resemblance. The first element of the name is the god *Bel*,—this I consider to be certain; the second element I read doubtfully *adonim*, and the third is sometimes written *sa* or *shu*, and sometimes *rim*, these two words being probably synonyms[1]. If, therefore, this king be really the Sennacherib of sacred

---

[1] I proceed to give a brief analysis of this name. The first element is either ➤➤⟩ ⟨⟨⟨ or ➤➤⟩ ➤⟨⟨ ⟨➤⟩⟩, that is, it is the name of the god who was represented by either one or the other of these groups, and that god was undoubtedly בל or Belus; for the monogram ➤⟨⟩⟩⟩, which is a contraction of ➤➤⟩ ➤⟨⟨, is used at Behistun for the last syllable of the name of Naditabir, and ➤⟨⟨, moreover, denoting simply a lord or master, like the Hebrew בצל, is replaced in the Khorsabad Inscriptions by the forms of ➤◄ ➤⟩, ➤◄ ⟨⟩⟩, or ➤◄ ⟨⟨➤⟩⟩, all of which give the sound *Bel*, and by the fuller form of ⟨⟨ ➤⟩⟩ ⟨⟨➤⟩⟩ or *Bil*, upon Bellino's Cylinder. My own belief is, that ➤⟨⟨ is a simple *b*, and is used by abbreviation for *Bel*, both as the name of the god, and to express the word "lord." The character ⟨➤⟩⟩ invariably joined to the ➤⟨⟨ in Assyrian, and usually in Babylonian (but not always—compare the names of the witnesses to the contracts published by Grotefend, which mean "the servant of Bel," "given by Bel," "devoted to Bel," &c.), is phonetically an *l*, and is thus either used to complete the phonetic expression of the name, or, as I think more probable, to distinguish the male deity ➤⟨⟨ ⟨➤⟩⟩ Belus, from the female Beltis, or ➤⟨⟨ ➤⟩⟩⟩. I am not sure of the phonetic power of ⟨⟨⟨ in Babylonian. Curiously enough, in Median it does, I think, actually represent *s-n*, but it would seem to be a simple *b* or *b-s* in the other alphabet; for the groups ➤⟩⟩ ⟨⟩➤ ⟩,

and profane history, we must believe the name, in its popular and phonetic form, to be as yet undiscovered. The few records, at the same time, of the Koyunjik king, that have been as yet alone found, coincide in some degree with our historical notices of Sennacherib. On the great tablet at Bavian the Koyunjik king records his conquest of Babylon, which agrees sufficiently well with the statement of Abydenus and Alexander Polyhistor that Sennacherib thus inaugurated his reign[1]. In an inscription upon one of the bulls at Koyunjik

⟬cuneiform⟭ and ⟬cuneiform⟭ are phonetically identical, and at Khorsabad, in Pl. 80, l. 7, ⟬cuneiform⟭ is used for the initial character of the name of Media.

The second element of the name I am considering is ⟬cuneiform⟭, and I do not pretend to have any satisfactory grounds for reading it as *adonim*. The ⟬cuneiform⟭ or ⟬cuneiform⟭ has, however, I think, almost certainly the phonetic value of *m* or *v*, and I have spoken of the other characters in my note on the name of Sardanapalus.

The third element is ⟬cuneiform⟭ or ⟬cuneiform⟭, and, either as ideographs or phonetic groups, both these terms are strange to me; the latter group, however, has certainly the power of *r-b*, and would thus answer well enough for the concluding syllable of the name of Sennacherib.

Since writing the above, I have received Dr. Hincks's paper on the Khorsabad Inscriptions, and have attentively read his remarks on the presumed name of Sennacherib, contained in pages 25 and 35. I am bound to say that I can discover no authority whatever for reading ⟬cuneiform⟭ or ⟬cuneiform⟭ as *sen*, beyond the clue afforded by the value of the character in Median, and in this case I certainly think that clue fallacious. I must further add, with all due deference to Dr. Hincks's happy talent of solving enigmas almost by intuition, that ⟬cuneiform⟭ or ⟬cuneiform⟭ is not *ci-na*, but *Bel* (the *n* being substituted for *l*, as usual); that ⟬cuneiform⟭ is not *θā* in Median, but *sar*, being in fact the Assyrian ⟬cuneiform⟭ and Babylonian ⟬cuneiform⟭; that "from" in Median is simply ⟬cuneiform⟭ *mer*, the preceding ⟬cuneiform⟭ being the case inflexion, answering to the Turkish *ñeñg*; that ⟬cuneiform⟭ has in Babylonian the power of *m* rather than of *gi*, and that I believe the plural sign ⟬cuneiform⟭ to have a similar phonetic value of *im*, though the *m* probably lapses before a following *n*. After reading, indeed, and carefully considering all Dr. Hincks's arguments, I remain as incredulous as ever of the identity of the Koyunjik king with the Sennacherib of Scripture.

[1] See Cory's Fragments, pp. 6, 16, 63.

here is also a notice of this king's conquest of Sidon, and the name of the monarch who was conquered may perhaps be read as Ithobal[1].

It would seem highly probable that it was upon the same expedition into Phœnicia that the triumphal tablet was engraved at the Nahar el Kalb, and as the Assyrian monarch has there apparently retorted upon Egypt the boast of foreign conquest, the circumstances would seem particularly applicable to the great expedition of Sennacherib, which is alluded to both in Holy Writ and by Herodotus, and in which Josephus states that the Assyrian king not only took Ashdod and Pelusium, but also ravaged Lower Egypt[2].

Of the son of this king very little indeed is known from the inscriptions, but the two first elements of his name are identical with those that occur in the name of Sardanapalus, and thus read, according to my phonetic system, Assar-adan, which represents as near as possible the Esarhaddon of Scripture[3].

These are the immediate points connected with the inscriptions of the Khorsabad dynasty, which seem to me to be favourable to the identification of the line with the Scriptural kings, Shalmaneser, Sennacherib, and Esarhaddon. The general position which would also lead to the same conclusion, and which of course is that usually put forward, is, that monarchs of such power as those who overran Palestine, and carried the Ten Tribes into captivity, must needs, in a country where sculptured slabs and votive bulls appear to have answered the same purpose as our modern gazettes and bulletins, have left some memorials of their sway,—while, if any such memorials do exist amongst the relics that have lately been disinterred, the inscriptions of Khorsabad and Koyunjik are those alone which will answer.

It is no love of paradox that makes me resist this accumulation of evidence. It is merely that calmness of research which refuses to take up an hypothesis, however tempting, before the arguments which exist against it are either removed or overcome. These arguments I will now briefly enumerate:—

1stly.—The nomenclature. I cannot reconcile it to my under-

[1] See British Museum series, Pl. 61, l. 8. The name of the king of Sidon, much mutilated, and consequently of a very uncertain orthography, is found at the end of line 7 in Pl. 59 of the British Museum series.

[2] Compare with Josephus, Ant., lib. x. c. 1, the passage in Herodotus, lib. ii. c. 141, and Isaiah c. xx. v. 4, where, however, the subjugation of Egypt would seem to be attributed to Sargon or Shalmaneser rather than to Sennacherib.

[3] The only Inscription known of this king is that published in Pl. 19 of the British Museum series.

standing that names which read Arko-tsin and Bel-adonim-sha
denote the two kings Shalmaneser and Sennacherib. The name of
the latter king, indeed, is given, without any sensible variation, by
the sacred historians, by Herodotus, and by the Chaldee annalists
Berosus and Abydenus, and it is to me incredible, or at any rate
inexplicable, that a title, which is thus shown to have been so universally known, should have been replaced on the monuments by a
perfectly different appellation.

2ndly.—The synchronism of the Khorsabad king with Hoshea,
king of Israel, obtained through the notice of Bocchoris, king of
Egypt, is by no means to be depended on. We cannot be sure, in
the first place, that Biarku is the same name as Bocchoris, written in
Egyptian Pe-hur (or, according to Mr. Birch, Bak-har); and even if
the names be identical, the allusion will more probably be to Pe-hur
or Bak-har, the fifth king of the twenty-first dynasty, than to the
Saite Bocchoris of the twenty-fourth dynasty, whose name never
occurs in the hieroglyphs, who reigned but a very few years, and
who, as an usurper, would hardly have been recognised by the
Assyrian monarch as king of Egypt; especially in records which,
if the two kings had really been Shalmaneser and Bocchoris, as there
was an interval of at least eight years between the war with Egypt
and the date of the inscription, must have been engraved several years
after the Ethiopian dynasty had succeeded to power[1]. According,
moreover, to the best Egyptian chronology, Bocchoris, the predecessor
of Sabaco, cannot have been upon the throne of Egypt at any period
of Shalmaneser's reign[2].

As far as the campaigns are concerned, I attach no great importance
to the coincidences I have noticed, for almost every Assyrian monarch
of note warred in Syria, and the conquests, therefore, of Ashdod and
Sidon may apply to any king of the dynasty, as well as to Shalmaneser
and Sennacherib. Independently of this, there is no notice of the
Khorsabad king's siege of Samaria, nor of the Koyunjik king's wars

---

[1] Bocchoris reigned but six years, according to Manetho; and as the war
between Assyria and Egypt is distinctly placed in the seventh year of the Nineveh
reign, he could not have been upon the throne when Khorsabad was built, which
records events as late as the fifteenth year of the same reign. The date of the
Egyptian war is fixed in the No. II. series of the Khorsabad Historical Annals
(see Pl. 75), where the events are chronicled according to their yearly order, while
the number 15 is found in the phrase "from the commencement of my reign to
the 15th year," which heads each section of the annals.

[2] I state this on the authority of the Chevalier Bunsen, who has kindly allowed
me to inspect his MS. Chronological Tables.

with Egypt, events which, if the monarchs recorded were really Shalmaneser and Sennacherib, could hardly fail of being recorded.

These, however, are negative arguments. I will now state what I regard as positive evidence against the identification. There are, in the first place, many records of kings in Assyria, who were certainly later than the builders of Khorsabad and Koyunjik. One of these, whose annals are stamped on a clay cylinder in the British Museum, seems to have warred on fully as great a scale as his predecessors; he describes his conquest of Syria and Phœnicia, of Asia Minor, of Babylonia, of Susiana, of Media[1]. A second, whose history is found on a slab at Nimrud brought from some other locality, mentions nearly a hundred cities which he had brought under subjugation to the Assyrian yoke[2]. There are other kings who must be placed in the same category: the monarch recorded on Lord Aberdeen's black stone, and another whose name occurs upon a slab found in the upper debris at Koyunjik. The proof of their being posterior to the son of the Koyunjik king is, in my opinion, almost positive; and if, therefore, the builders of Khorsabad and Koyunjik were really the monarchs mentioned in Scripture, who, I ask, can be the later sovereigns? There could have been no Assyrian king who carried his arms to the vicinity of Palestine, between Esarhaddon and Nebuchadnezzar, and the record, therefore, on the cylinder to which I have alluded, is, to my mind, fatal to the identification of the Khorsabad and Koyunjik kings with Shalmaneser and Sennacherib.

There is still another circumstance, which bears, I think, even more strongly against the identification. The south-west palace of Nimrud, which Mr. Layard somewhat too hastily ascribed to the son of the Koyunjik king, may, it seems to me, be attributed with safety to some monarch belonging to a line distinct from that of the Khorsabad and Koyunjik kings. There is, it is true, a pair of bulls, found in the palace, bearing the name of Assar-adan-assar, who was grandson of the Khorsabad king, and son of the builder of Koyunjik; but this is no proof whatever that Assar-adan-assar was the founder of the edifice. The bulls may very well have been brought from some other locality to ornament the new edifice; and the edifice itself must, I repeat, have been the work of some monarch of a different line, for the greater part of it is constructed of slabs brought from the centre palace of Nimrud; and the annals engraved upon those slabs,—the

[1] See British Museum Series, from 20 to 29 inclusive; and see particularly l. 53 sqq. of Pl. 22 for the proof of posteriority.

[2] See Plates 17 and 18 of the British Museum series. These Inscriptions are described in some detail in their proper places.

annals, be it observed, of the Khorsabad king,—have been intentionally defaced and destroyed by the new architect. Mr. Layard was not aware to what period these annals referred, as the name of the king is wanting, but they are now proved, by their contents, to belong to the builder of Khorsabad, the names of most of his antagonists and tributary kings being found upon them[1]. It is not credible that a grandson would have thus desecrated the monuments of his grand-father. Taking into consideration, indeed, the ancestral reverence of the Orientals, I feel persuaded that the wanton destruction of the annals of the Khorsabad king must have been the act of some member of an entirely different family. This family I can only conjecture to have been the lower dynasty of Assyria mentioned in Scripture, and if that be admitted, it will follow as a necessary consequence that Khorsabad and Koyunjik must be referred to the upper and original royal line[2].

Having thus stated the principal arguments both for and against the identification of the kings of Khorsabad and Koyunjik with the Biblical Shalmaneser and Sennacherib, I venture to observe, that although I am still disposed to assign a much higher antiquity to the restored dynasty of Nineveh, placing the accession of the Khorsabad king at least two centuries before the time of Hoshea and Hezekiah, I would still recommend all parties to refrain from coming to a deci-sion, until fresh elements of inquiry be obtained, either by the dis-covery of new inscriptions in Assyria, or by a more critical acquaint-ance with the contents of those that we already possess.

I will now briefly notice the Inscriptions of Khorsabad. They are of four classes:—

First, there is the Standard Inscription, which contains the names and titles of the king, and a list of the principal tribes and nations subject to Assyria; and appended in several instances is a notice of the building of the city of Khorsabad, "near to Nineveh and after

---

[1] See, amongst others, Bisri of Shaluma and Tarkheler of Taguma, named in lines 11 and 12 of the British Museum series, Pl. 50, No. 1, both of these chiefs being well known in the Inscriptions of Khorsabad.

[2] Whilst these pages are passing through the press, I learn from Mr. Layard that he has found the names of two new kings at Nimrud, the son and grandson of the king who dedicated the bulls in the south-western palace; and that in exca-vating a mound four miles to the north-west of Koyunjik, he has met with two other names, belonging apparently to monarchs posterior to the Khorsabad family. All these discoveries furnish additional arguments for supposing the builders of Khorsabad and Koyunjik to be anterior to the age of Shalmaneser and Sen-nacherib.

the manner of Egypt," together with a prayer to the gods for its protection.

The Second class consists of the long Inscriptions on the Votive Bulls, which, without being strictly historical, go into much greater detail regarding the constitution of the empire, and name the various kings and chieftains subdued by the Assyrian monarch. There are also in these inscriptions very elaborate notices of the Assyrian Pantheon.

The Third, or historical class, consists of the slabs surrounding the sculptured halls, interposing between the bas-reliefs which represent the battles and sieges recorded in the inscriptions. Some of these records are in the form of regular yearly annals, whilst in others the entire history of the monarch's reign is given as a continuous narrative, without being interrupted by divisions of time. Of the latter class of inscriptions, the Hall marked No. 10 in the French plates contains an admirable specimen, the writing being almost perfect throughout the entire series, and forming, I should think, as complete and elaborate an historical record, as was ever executed upon stone. In some of these inscriptions the geographical detail is quite bewildering. In the series, indeed, which surrounds the Hall No. 2, there must be, at least, 1000 names of districts and cities, overrun or occupied by the Assyrian king[1].

The inscriptions of the Fourth class are those on the back of the slabs, which were never intended to be seen; they are strictly religious, containing no geographical notices whatever, but merely noticing the building of Khorsabad by the king, and invoking the gods to extend their protection to the city[2].

[1] In the second and third class of Inscriptions I should observe that the building of the city of Khorsabad is also commemorated at the conclusion of the historical and geographical detail.

[2] I observe that Dr. Hincks (p. 41 of his pamphlet on the Khorsabad Inscript.) infers, from the absence of the title "King of Babylon," and the omission of all notice of Nebo, the special divinity of Babylonia, on the Khorsabad reverses, that these Inscriptions were executed at an early period of the monarch's reign, before his conquest of Babylon, and were subsequently rejected: but I can hardly adopt this view of the matter. When the king styles himself , I understand him to include Babylonia. Immediately after proclaiming his titles, he further invokes the tutelary gods of Mesopotamia (or 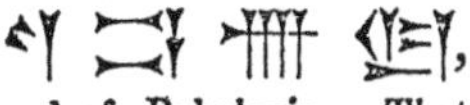, the special name of the Euphrates in a later age) and of Babylonia. That Nebo is omitted in recapitulating the gods is true, but so also are omitted both Assarac and Sut, and the former was certainly the special divinity of Assyria. That, however, which to my mind seems to prove that the Inscriptions on the

I will now give a general sketch of the contents of the Historical series of Inscriptions. Arko-tsin, (the ordinary phonetic form of the Khorsabad king's name,) terms himself the king of Assyria and Babylonia, and of two provinces, of which the titles are usually given as Saberi and Hekti, and which may be understood to denote that portion of Upper Asia immediately to the eastward of the valley of the Tigris[1]. His three special divinities, those whom he addresses in every inscription immediately after proclaiming his own titles, are Assarac, Nebu, and Sut[2].

A catalogue then follows of geographical names, which appear intended to mark the limits only of the Assyrian dominion, rather than to furnish a complete view of all the tributary provinces[3].

It commences with the passage,—" From Yetnán[4], a land sacred to the god Husi[5], as far as Misr and Misek, (or Lower and Upper Egypt,)

reverses and on the faces of the slabs at Khorsabad were executed at the same time, and that the only difference is of a religious character, is that they both equally refer to the building of Khorsabad, which indeed was the special object they were designed to commemorate, and which assuredly was a work undertaken at a late period of the monarch's reign. At the end of the Inscription on the Khorsabad reverses there is an invocation to "the great gods inhabiting heaven and earth, and the gods inhabiting this city,"—Khorsabad being then built.

[1] I conjecture that the name Hekti, or rather perhaps Haikdi, may be connected with the Armenian Haik; but the title would seem, from the geographical indications, to be applicable to Adiabene rather than to Armenia Proper.

[2] Sut was known to the Egyptians as a god of the Semite nations. Mr. Birch suggests an identity with Sadak (Συδύκ of Sanchoniathon), or even with Satan (see Trans. Royal Soc. of Lit., 2nd ser., Vol. II. p. 338); but I would prefer comparing the Babylonian Hercules, whom Berosus, quoted by Agathias, names Σάνδης; for the initial character of the name ⟨— has the primary power, I think, of Sar or San, and is only used for su by a softening of the liquid. I have not been able to recognize the emblems of Sut, on the Cylinders, though the name is far from uncommon.

[3] It is of some interest to compare the geographical catalogues that occupy so conspicuous a place in the Standard Inscriptions of Nimrud and Khorsabad with certain passages of the Greek authors referring to the same subject. I allude to the list of the conquests of Ninus given by Diodorus Siculus, on the authority of Ctesias, and to the statement of the Assyrian boundaries which, according to Polyænus, was found on the famous monument of Semiramis, (see Diod. Sic. lib. ii. pp. 64, 65, and Polyæn. lib. vii. c. 25). It can hardly be doubted, I think, although the individual Greek names are not to be recognized in the Inscriptions, that both Ctesias and Polyænus must have had some knowledge of the geographical matter contained in the Assyrian tablets.

[4] Compare the יקנען of Joshua xv. 23.

[5] The god whose name is written indifferently ◁𝅥 ⟨𝅥⊢ and ⊨𝅥𝅥𝅥⊨ ⟨𝅥⊣, or simply ◁𝅥 or ⊨𝅥𝅥𝅥⊨, is, I feel pretty sure, "the sun;" for it is imposs-

Maratha or Acarri[1], (which was the sea-coast of Phœnicia,) and the land of the Sheta."

The countries are afterwards mentioned in succession, of Media, Vakana, (perhaps Hyrcania,) Ellubi, Rasi, and Susiana; and the list closes with a multitude of names of tribes and cities which belong to Susiana, Elymais, and Lower Chaldæa, and the positions of which are illustrated by their contiguity to the great rivers Tigris, Eulæus, and Pasitigris[2].

ible otherwise to explain the phrase which occurs in almost every Inscription, to indicate the extension of the Assyrian sway, and which must needs be translated, I think, "from the land of the rising to the land of the setting sun," or "from east to west" (see British Museum series, Pl. 1, l. 14; Pl. 17, l. 2; Pl. 33, l. 5; Pl. 73, ll. 5—7, &c. &c.).   Another name for the god Husi is [cuneiform] [cuneiform] or [cuneiform] [cuneiform], which, as it may read Shemir or Semir, has some resemblance to Semiramis.   The same orthography, however, would answer to *Shemes* on the one side (*r* and *s* interchanging), and to *Sur* on the other (the labial being softened to a vowel), and both of these are well-known names for the sun.   Since writing the above, I have observed that Dr. Hincks (Khors. Ins., p. 24) considers the god [cuneiform] to be undoubtedly "the moon."   I suspect, however, that the crescent figured on the Cylinders refers to the god [cuneiform] [cuneiform] [cuneiform], who is joined with [cuneiform] [cuneiform] or "the sun," as an object of worship.   Compare the Cylinders numbered 23, 25, 30, 57, &c., with the passages on Bellino's large Cylinder, side 2, ll. 40 and 42, where [cuneiform] [cuneiform] and [cuneiform] [cuneiform] [cuneiform] are associated.   At Behistun, at any rate, [cuneiform] is never used for "a month;" the determinative monogram for that period of time is [cuneiform], as in British Museum series, Pl. 53, l. 32, and in all the contracts published by Grotefend.

[1] Maratha and Acarri are Μάραθος and Ἀκή, or Acre, as already explained.

[2] The names are given in greater or less detail in the different Inscriptions. The tribes which are usually mentioned, and which are particularly stated to be "Arabs" ([cuneiform] [cuneiform] [cuneiform]), are, along the banks of the Tigris, the Yetah, the Rebiah (ربیة), the Kheril, the Lemdod (compare אלמודד, and perhaps modern Lemlun), the Khamran (compare Καμαρίνη applied by Eupolemıs to Ur of the Chaldees), the Hubil (Heb. עובל), the Rahua, and the Luhti; and along the rivers of Susiana (which are identified quite positively by the ample geographical notices contained in Pl. 66 of the Khorsabad series), the Tebilu, the Akindara (or Akirdaru), the Bildu (?), and the Sati.   Of the cities mentioned in this list, those of most consequence, as we learn from other notices, are Taha Dunis, Beth Takkara, and Beth Eden, upon the sea coast.   On reading Dr. Hincks's paper on the Khorsabad Inscriptions, I find that he has transferred these

Then occur the annals, which are said to extend from the commencement of the king's reign to his fifteenth year[1].

The first campaign noticed is against Halubi-nerus, (?) king of Susiana; he was defeated, and 27,800 of his men, 200 of his captains, and 50 of his superior officers were carried into captivity.

The second campaign was against certain tributaries of the king of Egypt, and as in this passage, (which is repeated however in several of the halls,) occurs the only mention of the Egyptian monarch's name, I will give the sense as literally as I am able[2].   " Khanan, king of the city of Khazita, and Shelki, of the tribe of Khalban, belonging to the country of Misr (or Egypt), prepared their forces for battle in the city of Rabek. They came against me, and I fought with them and defeated them[3]." The punishment to which the two chiefs were doomed is given, and the inscription then continues:—" I received the tribute of Biarku or Biarhu, king of Misr," certain unknown articles, coming from the countries of Harida and Arbaka, " gold, Asbatera, (perhaps tin,) horses, and camels." Now the name of Rabek, which is constantly made use of in connexion with the tributaries of Misr, is an almost exact translation of Heliopolis, the city of the sun.   Biarku may be Pe-hur or Bocchoris, and Misr certainly, I think, represents

names from the Persian Gulf to the Mediterranean, applying titles which really belong to tribes and cities of Susiana and Lower Chaldæa to the Syrian districts of Ituræa, Galilee, Lebanon, and Hauran.   He has been led into this error, I presume, from overlooking the names of Susiana, ⟨XᚈЄ Єᚈ ⟨ᚈ=ᚈ or ᚈᚈᚈ ⟨⟨=ᚈᚈ ⟶ᚈ⟨, (the latter being perhaps a plural form equivalent to the Heb. עילם), and from his ignorance that the name ⊁⊹ ⊹⊏⊲ Є⊲ denoted the Tigris.

[1] In this sketch, I follow the order observed in the sculptures which surround Salle X., the events of the king's reign being there given in a sort of continuous narrative, without any reference to yearly dates.   In Salles II. V. and XIV., the same events are chronicled, but they are given in greater detail, and strictly in the form of annals.

[2] The account of receiving tribute from Egypt is given in a somewhat fuller manner in Salle II. No. 11, Pl. 75; but the writing is too much mutilated to render the notice of any great value.   The name of the Egyptian king, however, is written Biarka, rather than Biarku, the final ⊏ᚈᚈᚈ⊏ being dropped.

[3] In the annals given in Salle II., the campaign here noticed is spoken of in the second year of the king's reign, while the Egyptian tribute was not received till the seventh year; yet in the passage, as it occurs in Salle X. (Pl. 145, 2, ll. 1—3), the two events are most certainly connected.

Egypt[1]; but is it not strange to find horses and camels among the tribute of Egypt, the former animal having been apparently unknown in that country until the eighteenth dynasty, and having been subsequently so rare an object as to be received in tribute from the nations of the east?[2]

The next campaign is against Kehek, the king of Shenakti, a city which is usually mentioned in conjunction with Ashdod, and which must therefore have been situated on the sea-coast of Phœnicia, being perhaps the same place as Askelon; and here occurs a notice which I conceive to be of extreme interest. After the city of Shenakti was taken from Kehek, it was presented by the Assyrian king to Methati

---

[1] That the Ra-bek of the Inscriptions must represent On or Heliopolis is rendered almost certain by the name of the Syrian Heliopolis, which was vernacularly termed Baal-bek, the Phœnician Baal being exactly equivalent to the Egyptian Rá, or "the sun." Herodotus, in the same way, names the city of Venus Ατάρβηχις; and Ptolemy, for the city of Ammon, has Παχναμουνις. ΒΛΚΙ indeed, is still retained in the Coptic to denote "a city," and the Coptic translator, therefore, of the Bible explains the Hebrew אָן or בֵּית שֶׁמֶשׁ, which is the Greek Heliopolis, by ΒΛΚΙ ᚎ⳿ΦΡΗ. This determination of Heliopolis as the Egyptian capital, will agree sufficiently well with the synchronism which I have throughout sought to establish between the Khorsabad royal line and the twenty-first dynasty of Manetho; for that dynasty was the first that established its seat of government in Lower Egypt. I do not pretend, at the same time, to give the identification of Biarku with Pe-hur, the fifth king of the dynasty, as anything more than a conjecture. The name ⟨cuneiform⟩ or simply ⟨cuneiform⟩, will read Bianka as well as Biarka, for the ⟨cuneiform⟩ n and ⟨cuneiform⟩ r interchange perpetually; and Bianka resembles Pi-anch (as the name is read by Bunsen), the sixth king of the dynasty, rather than his immediate predecessor, Pe-hur; and, as far as the chronology is concerned, one king will suit as well as the other.

[2] The animals mentioned in this passage, which I have translated by camels, may possibly be elephants; for the epithet "with the double back," used in the epigraphs on the Obelisk, and applied especially to the camel depicted in the sculpture, is here omitted. It appears to me, indeed, extremely probable that as the elephant and the camel are denoted by nearly similar terms in the old Gothic and Slavonian tongues (the original signification perhaps being "the big animal"), so the Assyrian *Habba* (compare Sans. *ibha*; Egypt. *abu*; Heb. *habbim*, &c. &c.) may have been applied to the two animals indifferently. It is, at any rate, natural enough to find elephants included amongst the tribute of Egypt, whereas the export of camels from that country to Assyria can only be explained by their having been imported in the first instance from India. The attribution of the name of *Habba* to the elephant, as well as to the camel, will also render it probable that the same word applied to a natural object may signify "a forest" rather than "a desert." There are, however, some very obscure questions of etymology connected with this subject, which it would be inconvenient to discuss at present.

of Atheni[1], and to increase the probability of our having thus the earliest notice of Athens upon record, I must add, that in the general inscriptions which give a synopsis as it were of the historical data, the city of Shenakti is said to be held by the Yavana. That the latter name, moreover, really refers to the Ionians, there cannot be any doubt, for it occurs precisely with the same orthography at Behistun; and I confess, therefore, that I am half inclined to regard Methati of Atheni as Melanthus of Athens; the general views which I entertain of Assyrian chronology agreeing well enough with the date of Melanthus, who reigned, it may be remembered, very shortly after the first emigration of the Ionian families to Athens; at any rate we have here, I think, a notice of an Athenian chief presented with a Phœnician sea-port by the Assyrian king, for naval assistance probably rendered during the siege of the place.

The fourth campaign was against Amris, king of Tubal, who seems to have been supported by Arrah, king of Ararat, and by Meta, king of Misek, and also by the tribe of the Amorites, here called Amári. The conjunction of Tubal, Misek, and Ararat, certainly reminds one of Meshec and Tubal, who are always united in Ezekiel with Gog and Magog, and who are supposed to represent tribes in the northern part of Asia Minor. Meta, however, king of Misek, is often spoken of in connexion with Misr and the city of Rabek, where he seems to have generally resided; the two countries are always more or less associated, and if Misr therefore be Lower Egypt, Misek must of necessity be some country immediately contiguous; in all probability "the upper country" of the Hieroglyphs[2]. If this identi-

---

[1] The name of this chief is usually written at Khorsabad as 𒀭𒈾𒂊𒈾, but at Nimrud, in Inscriptions of the Khorsabad epoch, as 𒀭𒈾𒂊𒈾 (See British Museum series, Pl. 67, l. 1, where, however, the initial character is mutilated). From a comparison of the two forms, the orthography of *Methati* of *Atheni* seems to me undoubted.

[2] I have long considered the identification of the country of which the name is represented by 𒀭𒈾𒂊 or 𒀭𒈾𒂊 (or any of the intermediate forms) to be one of the most difficult points connected with the Khorsabad Inscriptions. It did at one time appear to me highly probable that Misr was " Lower Egypt," and Misek " Upper Egypt," the similarity of the names causing them to be united in the Hebrew dual מצרים ; but I have since found it impossible to apply to a monarch who reigned in that remote country the many geographical notices which connect Meta of Misek with Syria and Armenia.

fication also be correct, the tribe of Tubal must be located in Northern Syria, between Palestine and the Upper Euphrates.

These campaigns, I should add, are almost all described in the same terms; the king of Assyria defeats the enemy in the field, subjugates the country, sacrifices to the gods, and then generally carries off the inhabitants, with their most valuable effects, into captivity in Assyria; repeopling the country with colonists drawn from the nations immediately subject to him, and appointing his own officers and prefects to the charge of the colonists, and the administration of the new territory.

It would be uninteresting to follow these campaigns in any detail. I will merely mention the countries which were successively overrun; firstly, we have Hamath and its dependencies; Atesh, however, which occupied so conspicuous a place in the wars of Temen-bar II. in connexion with Hamath, no longer appearing, and the inference therefore being that it must have been destroyed in the interval between the eras of Nimrud and Khorsabad. We have then a most elaborate account of a campaign against Ararat and Minni, the king of the former country, whose name was Arrah, reminding one of the Ara Keghetsig, or "Ara, the beautiful," of Armenian history. The con-

I now conjecture the people of Misek to be the Mes-segem of the Hieroglyphs, or the Semite inhabitants of Southern Syria, immediately bordering upon Egypt (see Birch's remarks on this nation—Trans. of Royal Soc. of Lit. 2nd series, Vol. II. p. 321), and it seems to me far from improbable that Adonibezek, whom the Israelites met on their first entrance into Palestine, and who was evidently very powerful (Judges i. 4—9), may have been king of the same people, Bezek and Misek being orthographically one and the same. There will still, however, be considerable difficulty in reconciling with a Syrian monarch the many Egyptian notices that refer to Meta; for he is described in some passages, according to the readings which seem to me most probable, as "residing in the city of Rábek, and administering the country of Misr."

I find from Dr. Hincks' paper on the Khorsabad Inscriptions, which has appeared since the above notes were written on Misr and Misek, that he reads the names ⟨𒀭 𒂍𒅆 𒅀 𒌋 𒈾 𒌍𒁹 𒆠𒂗 as "Gita of Kush," and actually makes use of this reading for chronological argument. That the letters ⟨𒀭 and its variant 𒅀 represent *m*, rather than *gi*, is proved by many examples at Behistun, and might have been inferred from the powers of the corresponding characters in Median. There cannot, therefore, by any possibility be an allusion to the Ζήτ of Africanus, and it appears to me equally impossible that 𒈾 𒌍𒁹 𒆠𒂗 should be pronounced Kush, whether by that name we may understand the African Æthiopia, or, as Dr. Hincks subsequently suggests, the Asiatic Susiana.

F

tiguous countries of Tsibasta and Hustisa are next subjugated. Yanaluh, king of Nahiri or Northern Mesopotamia, dwelling in the capital city of Hubiska, sent in his tribute. Assarelak of Taha-ela and Itti of Elabri are subsequently attacked and reduced, the king founding cities in these provinces for the Assyrian colonists whom he settled there to replace the population carried into captivity[1].

The next campaign was against Kharkhar or Persarmenia, and against Media, and in the latter country the various great cities that were taken, were dedicated to the Assyrian gods, and named after the principal members of the Pantheon, Taha-Nebu, Taha-Bel, Taha-Hem, and Taha-Ashtera.

Detailed accounts follow of wars against Rita of Ellubi, which appears to have been Southern Media, against Arazen of Mekhatseri, which was a city and dependency of Ararat[2], against Tarkhanzi of Mesda, Kanzinan of Khamána, and Tarkheler of Togoma.

The king afterwards marches into Syria and besieges Ashdod, ruled over by a king named Haleri, who after conducting the defence for some time, flies to Misr or Egypt, and the city falls. After this the war is resumed against Ararat and Ellubi, and Rita, the king of the latter country, is driven out and compelled to take refuge in Susiana.

The closing campaigns, which seem to have exceeded all others in importance, were against Susiana and Elymais, and against Babylonia

---

[1] To illustrate, or even to give an outline of the geography of the Khorsabad Inscriptions, would require more care and space than I can here bestow upon the subject. The names, indeed, of the cities, tribes, rivers, and towns belonging to each province are so numerous, and appear under such a variety of forms in the different Inscriptions of the period (the sculptured slabs of the centre and south-west Palace at Nimrud being referable to the same historical epoch as those of Khorsabad and Koyunjik), that their dissection and identification may be said to constitute a distinct study of itself. I shall reserve, therefore, the geographical detail of these Inscriptions for a future occasion.

[2] The name of Mekhatseri or Mezatseri, (for the name is written either with the guttural or sibilant,) might be conjectured to apply to Van itself; inasmuch as the god ►─┪ ►─ ⟨┤⊨┿, who was the special divinity of that place, and whom I am inclined to identify with the Armenian Anaitis, is mentioned in this passage at Khorsabad, and in this passage only, among the trophies brought away to Assyria after the conquest of Ararat. It is, I think, a remarkable circumstance, that so very few of the geographical names referring to Armenia and its dependencies in the Inscriptions of Nimrud and Khorsabad, should be found on the tablets of Van. I can only account, indeed, for the great discrepancy of nomenclature by supposing many centuries to have intervened between the two periods of history.

and Chaldæa, the whole of which countries were evidently very closely indeed connected. A multitude of tribes, cities, and chiefs are mentioned in describing these wars, which it would be wearisome to enumerate, though undoubtedly the information thus supplied will prove of the greatest value in illustrating the early geography of the provinces on the Persian Gulf.

There is still another expedition noticed against the seven kings of the Yakanatsi, who dwelt in the land of Yetnan, on account apparently of their refusing to pay the same tribute which had formerly been paid, the king says, " to the kings, my ancestors, who ruled over Assyria and Taha-Dunis." The rebellious tribes having been subdued were placed in bondage, some amongst the Khetta or Hittites, others amongst the Chaldees. Their gold, silver, and valuable property were carried off to Babylon, and they were themselves dispersed through the country as far as Beth Eden, and the Arab tribes who inhabited the district of Yetmira, dependent on Susiana.

After a further brief notice of Meta, king of Misek, the annals finish, and are followed by an account of the building of the city. " At that time," the king says, " among the people of the countries who were obedient to me, and who worshipped the gods Assarac, Nebu, and Sut, after the fashion of Egypt, and near to Nineveh, I built a city and named it Beth Arko-tsina[1] (or, to use the popular synonym, Beth Sargon), and I dedicated it to the gods, Bel, Shemir, Nebo, Hem, Seb," &c., &c. The remaining portion of the inscription is entirely religious and descriptive, relating to the embellishment of the city, and the institution of periodical festivals in honour of its tutelary deities.

I have thus given a brief sketch of the general purport of the

---

[1] In the few notes which I have been alone able to add to the present sheets in their passage through the press, since the publication of Dr. Hincks's Paper on the Khorsabad Inscriptions, I have purposely avoided all discussion upon points of etymology and grammar; for I could hardly hope in so hurried a manner to make myself at all intelligible. I cannot avoid however mentioning that the phrases 𒀀 𒁹 𒂖 𒐊 and 𒀀 𒁹 𒌋 𒂖 𒐊, which Dr. Hincks (p. 43) reads, "out of it I brought," and "out of them I brought," signify really, "I gave it the name," and "I named them," the forms of 𒈨 𒁹 𒂖 or 𒂖 𒁹 𒐊 being often substituted, which have the same sense, as derivatives from a root corresponding to זכר in Hebrew, and ذكر in Arabic.

inscriptions surrounding one of the halls at Khorsabad, and as all the other legends throughout the palace are, with little variation, either repetitions or amplifications of the several religious, historical, and geographical notices contained in this summary, I need not further discuss them.

One other subject only connected with the Inscriptions of Khorsabad requires a few remarks. These inscriptions furnish ample evidence of the introduction of a strong Scythic element into the population of Western Asia, during the period which elapsed between the eras of Khorsabad and Nimrud; but in what sense we are to understand Scythic, or rather to which family of nations the early Scyths are to be referred, is by no means clear. At Behistun there are repeated notices of the Sacæ, a name which it may be remembered, Herodotus says was applied by the Persians indiscriminately to all the Scythians. These Sacæ, indeed, are represented among the captives at Behistun, the last figure with the high cap, which Herodotus also remarks was peculiar to the nation, being Sakuka, the Sacan. Now in the Babylonian translation at Behistun, the term employed for Sacan is Tsimri, and this same term, unknown under Sardanapalus and his immediate line, runs as a general title through all the Assyrian inscriptions, from the age of Khorsabad downward[1]. There are thus the Tsimri of Khamána, the Tsimri of Beth Hebra, (which was a district I think of Syria,) the Tsimri of Tubal, the Tsimri of Babylonia, the Tsimri of Assyria. In fact, these Tsimri, I think, or nomade Scyths, are spoken of as the militia of the different provinces in contradistinction to the fixed agricultural peasantry. The question then arises, if the Tsimri can be the same as the Cymri or Celts of

---

[1] The name is found in two passages at Behistun, and is repeated three times at Nakhsh-i-Rustam with the same orthography of ⟨cuneiform⟩. In Assyrian, the last letter is dropped as superfluous, the character ⟨cuneiform⟩ representing the complete syllable *mer*, and the name, thus reduced to ⟨cuneiform⟩, may be observed in almost every Inscription of Khorsabad and Koyunjik and succeeding periods. I cannot be sure, as I have before remarked, that the character ⟨cuneiform⟩ represents *tsi* or *dsi*. This determination, indeed, depend on its resemblance to ⟨cuneiform⟩ or ⟨cuneiform⟩, and although the forms are often confounded, I see strong reason to doubt their phonetic identity. Very possibly ⟨cuneiform⟩ should be pronounced *Kimer* or *Cymr*, rather than Tsimri.

Europe. The Nakhsh-i-Rustam inscription divides the Sacæ into two great tribes, the Humarga, who are of course the 'Aμύργιοι of Herodotus[1], and the Tigrakhuda, or "bowmen," (as I now translate the title, rather than "dwellers on the Tigris);" but we gather nothing from these Persian names as to the great family of nations to which the Sacæ belonged. My own opinion is, that the terms Sacæ and Tsimri, which are perhaps synonyms, were applied to all the early warlike nomade nations, without any distinction whatever as to family. That there must have been a large Tartar population of Persia before the time of Cyrus, is proved by the so-called Median translations in the tri-lingual tablets, which are unquestionably written in a Tartar dialect; but I am by no means inclined to identify this population especially with the Sacæ. The Sacæ or Tsimri were, I think, the Eelyaut or nomades, as opposed to the fixed peasantry and they numbered probably in their ranks, Celts, Slavonians, and Teutons, as well as Tartars of all grades, from the primitive type of the Fin and Magyar to the later developed Turk and Mongolian. I may add, that these Tsimri are also mentioned by Jeremiah among the nations of Western Asia, in allusion apparently to the Sacæ who at that period held Northern Media and Assyria, and had even penetrated to Palestine and Egypt. The passage to which I allude is in the 25th verse of the 25th chapter, where the kings of Zimri are classed with the kings of Elam and the kings of the Medes.

I now pass on to Bel-Adonim-sha, son of the builder of Khorsabad. Of this king, unfortunately, very few historical inscriptions have been yet discovered; the only two, indeed, with which I am acquainted and which are at all legible, are, firstly, an Inscription engraved on the rock at Bavian[2], adjoining to the sculptures described by Mr. Layard on Mr. Ross's authority; and secondly, a legend on one of the votive bulls found at Koyunjik. •The former contains a very detailed account of Babylonia and Susiana; and in the latter, I find recorded the same conquest of Susiana or Elymais, together with the capture of

---

[1] This name, which is imperfect in the Persian copy, reads distinctly both in Median and Babylonian, as *Humawarga* or *Humurga*. I failed to recognize the name until I obtained Tasker's copy of the Nakhsh-i-Rustam Inscription, owing to the faulty representation of the final letter in the published Median text of Westergaard, and the Manuscript of Dittel.

[2] This Inscription, of which I saw an imperfect copy at Mosul, is repeated four times upon the rock at Bavian; and Mr. Layard having lately succeeded in taking copies of all the four legends, hopes, notwithstanding the mutilated condition of the writing, to be able, by comparing them together, to form one perfect and continuous text.

Sidon[1]. The inscription at the Nahr el Kelb also belongs to this king, and may be supposed therefore, with great probability, to commemorate the latter achievement, but unfortunately the cast of the inscription in the British Museum, for which we are indebted to Mr. Bonomi, is, beyond a few isolated words, altogether illegible. The ordinary Koyunjik Inscriptions are for the most part religious, and exceedingly difficult to make out; they are in fact, by far the most difficult inscriptions that have been yet met with in the Assyrian character[2].

I have already alluded to the opinion entertained by some people, that this king is Sennacherib, and have declared my own views to be against that identification. I will merely therefore here observe, that the notice of Sidon, instead of corroborating the Koyunjik king's claim to be regarded as Sennacherib, rather makes against it; for in the history of Sennacherib, as given by Josephus, the campaigns in Phœnicia, Egypt, and Judea are classed together, and Sidon therefore would hardly have been mentioned without some allusion being at the same time made to Egypt. According also to Scripture account, it is hardly credible that Sennacherib, after his disastrous retreat from Judea, should have had leisure to execute any tablet recording the conquest of Phœnicia, in the brief period which alone intervened between his return to Nineveh and his assassination in the temple of Nisroch.

Of the third king of this line we know positively nothing but the name; that name has been supposed by Mr. Layard to be identical with the name of the builder of the north-west Palace at Nimrud, but the identification seems to me to have been assumed on insufficient grounds. I read the one name as Assar-adon-pal or Sardanapalus, and the other as Assar-adon-assar[3].

---

[1] See Plate 61, of the British Museum series.

[2] Since the above was written, I have learnt from Mr. Layard that he has discovered a perfect, and apparently a very full historical Inscription of the Koyunjik king among the ruins of the palace which he has been excavating at that place. Such a discovery, which must almost certainly decide the question of this king's identity with Sennacherib, and which must further afford a most valuable addition to our general knowledge of Assyria, appears to me to be of far more importance than the mere laying bare of sculptured slabs, which, however interesting the design; neither furnish us with new ideas, nor convey any great historical truth.

[3] The third element of the one name is, I think, uniformly 〖glyph〗 or 〖glyph〗, and of the other 〖glyph〗, which I consider to be a contraction of 〖glyph〗. At the same time, I must repeat that very little confidence can be placed on the phonetic rendering of these names.

Before quitting the subject of the Khorsabad line of kings I must recur to Mr. Layard's late announcement, that in a perfect copy of the inscription, in the tunnel on the Zab river, he has found a notice of the royal ancestors of the Khorsabad king, ancestors who, singularly enough, are not even named in any other inscription of this monarch. Admitting the certainty of this discovery,—and the fragments of the tunnel Inscription already published are greatly in its favour [1],—I must of course modify the opinion I have advanced of the Khorsabad line having followed almost immediately on the royal line recorded at Nimrud; but I should still be inclined to attach a very moderate limit to the interval. If the Nimrud kings, indeed, should be assigned to the thirteenth or twelfth century before the Christian era, I would suppose the Khorsabad line to have flourished in the eleventh or tenth century.

I have already stated, that we know of many kings of Assyria posterior to the builders of Khorsabad and Koyunjik. The king whose actions are recorded on the cylinder in the British Museum seems to have been a not less celebrated warrior than Temen-bar himself; his expeditions are described against Sidon and Phœnicia, against Damascus and Tubal, against Ararat, Minni, and its dependencies, against Susiana or Elam, against Shinar and Chaldæa, with the famous cities of Beth Takkara and Borsippa, against the Arab city of Haduma, which, it is observed, Bel-Adonim-sha, the Koyunjik king, had subjugated in former times. It is further stated, how all the tribes were reduced who lined the Lower Tigris, and how the king afterwards pushed his arms into Media, and Central or perhaps Eastern Persia. Unfortunately this king is nameless; that is, the particular portion of the inscription which contains the name is destroyed; but he was certainly as celebrated a warrior as any of the monarchs who preceded him [2].

---

[1] The name of the father of the Khorsabad king is probably found at the commencement of the 5th line of Pl. 35 of the British Museum series. The initial letter or letters being lost, and some of the others being uncertain, I will not hazard a reading of the name; but I may observe that the fragments which remain are sufficient to show that the term appended to the royal title in the Khorsabad reverses is not a patronymic, as has been sometimes supposed. That term being compounded of the names of the gods, is probably an honorary epithet, but I know nothing certain regarding it.

[2] See British Museum series from 20 to 29. As the date of this Inscription is of great consequence to the argument about the identification of Sennacherib, and as the passage in Pl. 22, l. 53, imperfect as it is, may be considered inconclusive, or may even be supposed to refer the cylinder itself to the Koyunjik king, I think it as well to notice that the fragments which remain of the king's name in l. 1, Pl. 20,

Another cylinder of this class is in the possession of Col. Taylor, and, as far as I can ascertain from an impression of the writing, which I took many years ago, it contains the annals of a distinct king, not less elaborately described than those upon the Obelisk.

The black stone upon the table, belonging to the Earl of Aberdeen, names Akadunna,(?) who was king of Assyria and Babylonia, and who lived probably not long before the time of Nebuchadnezzar, as a Babylonian city is noticed which is of that epoch, and which is never mentioned in the earlier inscriptions[1].

One of the most powerful of all the kings, too, must have been a certain Akpalutakra,(?) of whom we have only one inscription, which however abounds in geographical detail. I place this king towards the close of the dynasty, as the names are found to be gradually approaching their Babylonian forms[2].

cannot possibly be brought to assimilate with 𒀭𒌋𒌋𒌋𒀀𒌋𒌋𒌋𒀭, and that there is the same disagreement between the name of the king of Sidon on the Cylinder, which is given in Pl. 20, l. 14, and again Pl. 21, ll. 40 and 50, and the king of Sidon, contemporary with the builder of Koyunjik, the fragments of whose name are found in l. 7 of Pl. 59. These points of evidence are of themselves sufficient to convince me that the Cylinder king must be posterior to the builder of Koyunjik; but the question can hardly be considered to be decided until the Cylinder annals have been compared with Mr. Layard's new historical Inscription from Koyunjik.

I now find that Dr. Hincks derives from this name of the king of Sidon an additional argument in favour of the identity of the Koyunjik king with Sennacherib; for he reads the name Abdistarti, and compares it with 'Αβδάσταρτος or עבד עשתרת, the name of a king stated by Menander to have ascended the throne of Phœnicia seven years after the death of Hiram, Solomon's contemporary, (see Khorsabad Inscriptions by Dr. Hincks, p. 69). I can hardly believe, however, that the Cuneiform name was read as Dr. Hincks supposes; for Ashtera, or Astarte, is always written in Assyrian as 𒀸𒀭 𒀭; and I find an equal difficulty in reconciling Menander's Abdastartus, who must have lived in the beginning of the tenth century B.C., with the usually received era of Sennacherib, which was at least 250 years later.

[1] I refer to the famous city inscribed on the Babylonian bricks, and on all the monuments of the age of Nebuchadnezzar, the name of which, 𒁲𒁲𒁲𒁲, I read doubtfully as Beth Digla, comparing the دَقْلَا of the Arabs (see line 16 of the last column of Lord Aberdeen's stone).

[2] See Plates 17 and 18 of the British Museum series, and compare l. 32 of Pl. 18, where the name 𒀭𒁹𒌍𒁹 is applied to the Euphrates, as at Behistun, instead of the old title of 𒁹𒁹 𒁹 or 𒁹𒁹 𒁹 𒁹.

There is still another king, named Akiba, of whom I saw an inscription at Koyunjik, found in the debris above the palace of Bel-adonim-sha; his wars were described in some detail with Ter-aman, king of Susiana, but there was nothing in the record to afford any clue to his historical identity[1].

Some of the monarchs whom I have thus mentioned, belong, I think, in all probability to the Lower Assyrian dynasty, or to that particular line mentioned in Scripture, but we must wait for fresh materials before coming to any definite conclusion even on this point.

The only approximate chronology that it is at all safe to assume at present is as follows. Herodotus gives for the duration of the Assyrian dominion in Upper Asia, 520 years, reckoning, as it would seem, from the defection of the Medes[2]. This defection of the Medes is, at the same time, a disputed point in chronology, and some even of the best chronologists maintain that the numbers of Herodotus, indicating a fixed epochal date, should be calculated from the Chaldæan era of Nabonassar[3]; but, whichever may be the correct explanation, the point of departure will, at any rate, almost certainly fall in the eighth century before Christ, and the Assyrian empire, therefore, may be considered, on the authority of Herodotus, to date from the com-mencement of the thirteenth century, B. C.[4]

[1] I must again notice the son and grandson of Assar-adon-assar, whose titles have been recently discovered by Mr. Layard, and also the two new monarchs, whose names he has found in excavating a mound to the north-west of Khorsabad. As I have not yet seen transcripts of these names, I can say nothing as to their possible phonetic reading.

[2] Lib. I. c. 95.

[3] With Niebuhr, I believe, originated this explanation of the numbers of Herodotus. The reasoning by which it is supported is considered by the German scholars to be conclusive, and Bunsen thus adopts throughout his work upon Egypt the dates which depend upon it (era of Nabonassar B.C. 747; commence-ment of Assyrian empire B.C. 1267) as established points in chronology.

[4] Since ancient history first occupied the attention of the learned of Europe, the chronology of the Assyrian empire has been one of the "quæstiones vexatæ" of classical literature. The long period and the short period, or the chronology of Ctesias and the chronology of Herodotus, have had their respective advocates, and authorities of almost equal weight have been marshalled upon either side. In confirmation of the dates of Herodotus, the Abbé Sevin has quoted Thallus, Appian, Dionysius of Halicarnassus, Porphyry, Macrobius, Africanus, and perhaps even Alexander Polyhistor; while Freret has brought to the support of Ctesias the evidence of Manetho, Plato, Aristotle, Pausanias, Cephalion, Castor, Æmilius Sura, Josephus, Ælian, Diodorus Siculus, Eusebius, Sulpicius Severus, Philo of Byblos, Eustathius, and Syncellus (compare the two articles in the fourth and seventh volumes of the Mémoires de l'Acad., XIIme. edit.). The school of Niebuhr implicitly follows Herodotus, regarding Alexander Polyhistor's sixth

Now, supposing that the records of Nimrud refer to an early period of the first, if not only, *imperial* dynasty, (and a fair examination of all the evidence doubtless leads to that conclusion,) the building of the north-west palace may be assigned to the end of the thirteenth or beginning of the twelfth century before the Christian era; and, as such a date would coincide with the twentieth dynasty of Egypt, the wars recorded on the Obelisk, in which the Assyrian arms were certainly pushed as far as Tyre, Sidon, and Byblus, would be explained by the depression under which Egypt suffered after the reign of Rameses III., the first king of the twentieth dynasty, and for the three following centuries. It is further to be observed, that the geographical indications are all in favour of this approximate chronology. The importance of the city of Atesh, the establishment of the Khetta in Southern Syria, the very nomenclature of the Phœnician ports,—Tyre, Sidon, Gubal or Byblos, Acarri or Acre, Beluta or Berytus, Arvad or Aradus,—constitute points of evidence which suit this period and no other[1]. I think, indeed, that almost all the Asiatic names which occur in the Egyptian records of the eighteenth and nineteenth dynasties, and in the wars of Rameses III., are to be found more or less modified in the Assyrian annals, and that the indications, therefore, of political geography may be held to restrict almost the age of the Nimrud obelisk to the twelfth century, B. C.

It must be quite unsafe to speculate on the causes and the duration of the interregnum, or at any rate of the unrecorded interval, which occurs between the Assyrian periods of Nimrud and Khorsabad. Possibly this period may be represented by the internal revolution which was described by Bion and Alexander Polyhistor, and which, according to their statement, changed the succession from the line of the Dercetades to the line of Beletaras, the officer who headed the revolt[2]. I cannot myself believe that there was any violent disruption of the line of Assyrian royalty, still less that the break in the annals was caused by foreign conquest. There may have been intestine troubles, which for a time prevented the extension of the Assyrian

dynasty of forty-five kings, as the only point of collateral evidence which is at all deserving of consideration, or which it may be worth while to compare even with the 520 years fixed by the Father of history; and, as far as Cuneiform research has hitherto extended, everything I think tends to confirm the German critique.

[1] Mr. Birch observes in his paper "On the Statistical Tablet of Karnac" (Trans. of Royal Soc. of Lit., 2nd series, Vol. II. p. 347), "During the nineteenth dynasty, Tyre and Sidon, Berytus, Aradus, Sarepta, and the Jordan, are mentioned; and under Rameses II. the empire had probably stretched as far as Beyrout, where it was met by the Assyrian boundary."

[2] See Agathias, Lib. II. p. 63.

arms to the westward, and put a stop to the erection of palaces and the engraving of inscriptions; but the Khorsabad king was certainly of the same race, probably of the same family; as the earlier monarchs of the Nimrud line; and I should not suppose that more than sixty or seventy years intervened between the two periods. If, then, the six continuous kings of the Nimrud line reigned, as I think, from about B. C. 1250 to B. C. 1100, and an interval were further allowed of seventy years after the suspension of the line, the era of the Khorsabad king would fall in about B. C. 1030, before the age of Solomon, and contemporary with a certain Pe-hor, of Egypt, who was the fifth king of the twenty-first dynasty, and who would thus represent the Biarku of the inscriptions, residing in the city of Rábek.

Before closing, I will rapidly run over the remaining subjects of interest connected with the Cuneiform Inscriptions. There are, it is well known, a series of inscriptions found at Van, and in the vicinity: These inscriptions I name Armenian. They are written in the same alphabet that was used in Assyria, but are composed in a different language,—a language, indeed, which, although it has adopted numerous words from the Assyrian, I believe to belong radically to another family, the Scythic[1]. There are six kings of the Armenian line following in a line of direct descent. I read their names as—1, Alti-bari; 2, Ari-mena; 3, Isbuin; 4, Manua; 5, Artsen; and 6, Ariduri(?) This family, which seems to have held extensive sway in Armenia, Asia Minor, and Northern Media, could have only, I think, risen into power on the decline of the Assyrian monarchy. On these grounds, then, which are further supported by certain points of intrinsic evidence contained in the inscriptions, I propose to assign the monuments of Van to the seventh and eighth centuries before Christ, supposing the kings who executed them to have been contemporaneous with those Medes who first threw off the Assyrian yoke.

I am not able, at present, to attempt a classification of the kings of Babylon, such as they are known from the various relics that we possess of them; nor, indeed, can I say, with any certainty, whether the kings recorded, with the exception of Nebuchadnezzar and his

---

[1] Dr. Hincks, it is well known, has published an elaborate paper on these Inscriptions in the ninth volume of the Society's Journal, and has endeavoured to prove that the language is Indo-Germanic. Admitting, however, the extreme value of the dissections contained in that paper, and greatly admiring, as I do, the sagacity that has determined the signification of so many words of which the phonetic rendering is quite erroneous, I cannot attach much weight to presumed grammatical affinities, when I know that the forms on which these affinities depend are in reality quite different from Dr. Hincks's readings.

father, may be anterior or posterior to the era of Nabonassar. The Babylonians certainly borrowed their alphabet from the Assyrians, and it requires no great trouble or ingenuity, at the present day, to form a comparative table of the characters; the hieratic signs, indeed, of the Assyrians and Babylonians differ more from the ordinary letters employed by them, than the alphabets of the two nations differ from each other.

The earliest Babylonian record that we have, is, I think, the inscription engraved on a triumphal tablet at Holwan, near the foot of Mount Zagros; it is chiefly religious, but it seems also to record the victories of a certain king, named Temnin, against the mountaineers. Unfortunately it is in a very mutilated state, and parts of it alone are legible[1].

On the relic called Michaux's stone, the purport of which is entirely religious, the name is Seb-pal-utakra, son of Beletsira, but I doubt the record being of royal origin. Upon a black stone in my own Cabinet, which appears to refer to the sale of certain lands upon the canal of Nimani, near Babylon, the king in whose reign the contract took place, is named Sut-athra-saram. The contracts upon the ordinary clay barrels, of which there are numbers in the museums of Europe, are usually of the Persian period, the documents dating from a certain year of the reign of Darius or Artaxerxes.

Perhaps the most interesting, however, of all the Babylonian monuments are the bricks. It was a custom, borrowed from Assyria, that the bricks used in building the ancient cities on the Lower Tigris and Euphrates should be stamped with the name and titles of the royal founder; and I should hope that ultimately specimens of these bricks, collected from every ancient site throughout Babylonia and Chaldæa (even if no other monuments should be found) would enable us to reconstruct the chronology of the country.

With regard to Babylonia proper, it is a remarkable fact, that every ruin from some distance north of Baghdad, as far south as the Birs Nimrud, is of the age of Nebuchadnezzar. I have examined the bricks *in situ*, belonging perhaps to one hundred different towns and cities within this area of about one hundred miles in length, and

---

[1] I discovered this tablet on the occasion of my last visit to Behistun, and with the help of a telescope, for there are no possible means of ascending the rock, succeeded in taking a copy of such portions of the writing as are legible. On the tablet itself, a figure, clad in sacerdotal costume and apparently a eunuch, is presenting to the monarch a throng of captives, who are chained together, their arms being bound behind them, and rings being fastened in their nostrils, to which the leading string is attached.

thirty or forty in breadth, and I never found any other legend than that of Nebuchadnezzar, son of Nabopalasar, king of Babylon[1]. Porter gives one legend of a king, Hem-ra-imris, upon a brick which was said to have been found at Hymar, near Babylon, but I should doubt its belonging to that site, as I have examined hundreds of the Hymar bricks, and have found them always to bear the name of Nebuchadnezzar. At the same time, it is impossible to believe that Nebuchadnezzar was really the first builder in Babylonia. As far as the town of Babylon is concerned, I admit without hesitation, that it owed its origin to that king, for the name is never once mentioned in the inscriptions anterior to the time of Nebuchadnezzar, and the monarch moreover says in Scripture,—" Is not this the great Babylon that I have built?" but with regard to the neighbouring city of Borsippa, which is certainly, I think, represented by the Birs Nimrud, there is evidence of its being the capital of Shinar, as early almost as the earliest Assyrian epoch. At any rate, Temen-bar, the Obelisk king, records his conquest of Borsippa in the ninth year of his reign, and the city is mentioned in every subsequent record. It would appear then, as the Birs Nimrud and the surrounding ruins are exclusively formed of bricks stamped with the name of Nebuchadnezzar, that in the earlier period, the people of Shinar could not yet have

---

[1] The principal ruins to which I refer in this part of Babylonia are, 1stly, At a spot on the Isháki canal, about fifteen miles north-east of Baghdad, where excavations are often made for the sake of obtaining bricks. 2ndly, At Baghdad itself, the right bank of the river within the town being formed for the space of nearly one hundred yards of an enormous mass of brickwork, which until lately was supposed to be of the time of the Caliphs, but which I found on examining the bricks to date from the age of Nebuchadnezzar. 3rdly, A large mass of mounds near the Khan Kahya on the road to Hillah. 4thly, Akkerkuf, called in the old Arabic works, " the Palace of Nimrud," and perhaps the Accad or Accar of Genesis. 5thly, Extensive ruins near Khan-i-Sa'ad, which formed the after site of Maiozamalca. 6thly, At Za'aleh near Musáib on the Euphrates. From this spot I obtained the black stone of Sut-athra-saram, and I have been assured that another inscribed tablet is to be found in the ruins, though as I once spent an entire day in vainly searching for the relic, I almost doubt its existence. 7thly, The famous city of Cutha, which I had the good fortune to discover in 1845, and which I have since repeatedly visited. The ruins are situated in Lat. 32° 41' 36", and Long. 44° 42' 46", and are almost equal to those of Babylon. From this city came the Cuthæans who colonized Samaria, and it was traditionally the scene of the early miracles of Abraham. The other cities of Nebuchadnezzar are at, Kalwádha, Hymar, Babylon, and Birs-i-Nimrud. I have no means at present of identifying with these sites the numerous cities named in the India-House Inscription, and on Bellino's Cylinder; nor indeed, can I venture to point out the emplacement of the two cities mentioned on the bricks, Beth Digla and Beth Dsida, (or Beth Jida), which seem to have been accounted the *chefs-d'œuvre* of Nebuchadnezzar.

adopted the Assyrian alphabet; and that Nebuchadnezzar, moreover, must have almost entirely rebuilt the city. This rebuilding, indeed, and especially the construction and dedication of the great temple, now represented by the Birs, is certainly noticed in the Standard Inscription of Nebuchadnezzar, of which the India-House slab furnishes us with the best and most perfect copy, and which is in fact a sort of Hieratic statistical charter, giving a detail of all the temples built by the king in the different towns and cities of Babylonia, naming the particular gods and goddesses to whom the shrines were dedicated[1]; and stating moreover a variety of matters connected with the support of the temples, and with the sacrificial and ceremonial worship of the kingdom, which I really cannot pretend at present to interpret with even approximate accuracy.

I may add, that in the old inscriptions, Babylonia is known by no other name than that of Shinar, a name which is not only familiar to us from Scriptural notices, but which has also been preserved in a fragment of the Greek historian Histiæus. I do not think that this name has any connexion whatever with the Singara of the lower Empire and modern Sinjar, and I should almost doubt even its identity with the Egyptian Saenkara, for I cannot believe that the Egyptian arms ever really penetrated to Babylonia. It is at any rate, I think, impossible, that the name of Babel should occur in an inscription of Thothmes III., for, as I have observed before, the title was locally unknown before the age of Nebuchadnezzar[2].

---

[1] In addition to those deities whom I have already had occasion to mention in speaking of the Assyrian Pantheon, I may notice the following gods named in Scripture, whom I have, I think, identified in the Inscriptions at Babylon. *Sheshach* and *Merodach,* 𒀭 𒀭 𒀭 and 𒀭 𒀭 𒀭 𒀭; *Gad* and *Minni,* 𒀭 𒀭, (see East India House Inscription, col. 4. ls. 38 and 52,) and 𒀭 𒀭 𒀭, (ditto, col. 1, l. 30). I suspect that the Succoth Benoth of Scripture, is the god (or goddess) whose name is ordinarily written 𒀭 𒀭 𒀭 𒀭, (see Bellino's Cylinder, side 1, l. 27, &c., and compare East India House Inscription, col. 4, l. 16, and Khorsabad Inscriptions, Pl. 87, l. 8; Pl. 152, l. 11, &c.), and it seems also far from improbable that 𒀭 𒀭 𒀭 𒀭 𒀭, (East India House Inscription, col. 4, l. 44,) may be the Biblical Leviathan, for on the cylinder numbered 76, in Cullimore's collection, this god is symbolized by a sort of marine monster.

[2] Since I penned note 3 to page 36, I have again carefully considered the

In the later Cuneiform Inscriptions, the ordinary name of Babylon seems to be Athra, which I conceive to be the name mentioned by Pliny, in his description of the Euphrates, when he says,—" The right branch of the river runs towards Babylon, formerly the capital of the Chaldees, and after traversing that city and also another which is called Otris, is lost in the marshes[1]."

whole question of the nomenclature of Babylon, and although in working out the argument I have followed a somewhat different course of induction from that pursued by Dr. Hincks, I have arrived at the same result. I have observed in the first place, from comparing the form 𒀭𒌷𒆠 with the form 𒀭𒆠, (see among other examples, East India House Insc., col. 4, l. 47, and col. 4, l. 28), that although in the former word an r (𒀭) is usually introduced, while in the latter, the n (𒀭) in every other example is replaced by l (𒀭 or 𒀭), still the resemblance of the two orthographies is sufficient to warrant the presumption of phonetic identity; and I have remarked in the second place, that the monogram 𒀭 does actually represent the same phonetic power as 𒀭, for not only is the plural form 𒀭 at Khorsabad constantly replaced by 𒀭, but at Persepolis this same character 𒀭 (imperfectly given by Westergaard, as 𒀭 or 𒀭, Plate xiv, a, line 10,) is used in the Babylonian translation of the Persian word *Duvarthim*, the term which it is intended to express being most assuredly *Báb*, "a gate," answering to בב in Chaldee, and باب in Arabic. I now therefore regard it as almost certain that the two forms of 𒀭 and 𒀭 were used indifferently to express phonetically the name of *Bábileh*, the remarkable and almost constant disagreement between them being the effect of a mere calligraphic fashion, rather than of any fixed alphabetic law; and I further conjecture, that the name orignated in the holy character of the city, the signification of it being "the Gate of God," or if we follow the mythology of Sanchoniathon, "the Gate of Ilus or Chronus." The objection, of course, which I have offered in the text to the possible occurrence of the name of Babel in the Hieroglyphic records must be now withdrawn, but I remain as incredulous as ever that the Egyptian arms could have really reached to the Lower Euphrates.

[1] See Pliny, lib. v. c. 21. Some of the manuscripts have Mothi instead of Otris. The form of 𒀭, which at Behistun is exclusively used for

Lower Babylonia or Chaldæa will probably furnish far more important materials for illustrating the ancient history of the country

Babylon, is first found, I think, in the East India House Inscription, where Nabo-palasar, the father of Nebuchadnezzar, is in two passages distinguished as king of 〔cuneiform〕 〔cuneiform〕, (see col. 7, ls. 11 and 48). Now that the sign of 〔cuneiform〕 has the phonetic power of *tr* or *thr*, is proved by its interchanging at Behistun with the letters 〔cuneiform〕 〔cuneiform〕 in the variant Babylonian orthographies of the Persian name Chitratakhma, as well as by its being often replaced in Assyrian by [the characters 〔cuneiform〕 〔cuneiform〕, (see amongst other passages, British Museum series, Pl. 7, l. 29); but I do not feel at all sure that as an ideographic monogram, it may not also have been pronounced Babel; just as the Assyrian monogram 〔cuneiform〕, representing ideographically the phonetic powers of 〔cuneiform〕 〔cuneiform〕 〔cuneiform〕, was, I think, pronounced Nineveh. At any rate, it is in this manner alone, that I can account for the uniform employment of the orthography in question at Behistun and Persepolis, in an age when the name of Babylon was universally, if not exclusively used upon monuments, and where the Persian and Median texts do actually give the true vernacular title.

Before I quit the subject of Babylon, I cannot avoid adding a few remaiks on the orthography of the name of Nebuchadnezzar, which Dr. Hincks, in p. 33 of his paper on the Khorsabad Inscriptions, seems to have involved in unnecessary obscurity. The only ideograph ever employed in writing this name is the monogram 〔cuneiform〕 or 〔cuneiform〕 for the name of the god Nebu. The remainder of the name in all its forms is phonetic; the third character, which has the form of 〔cuneiform〕 both on the bricks and on the East India House Inscription, but which is replaced by 〔cuneiform〕 at Behistun and on some other monuments, is the guttural *k* (〔cuneiform〕), optionally interchanging with a sibilant according to a law of Babylonian orthography; while the fourth character, which has also the form of 〔cuneiform〕 on the bricks, but which is more clearly represented as 〔cuneiform〕 in the E. I. H. Inscription, col. 1, l. 1, is used at Behistun in other names for *d*, and is, I believe, a mere variant of 〔cuneiform〕 or 〔cuneiform〕. The only other difficulty is in regard to the character 〔cuneiform〕, which has sometimes the power of *du*, sometimes of *dar*, and sometimes possibly of *dan*, for the final liquid in all characters of this class may be optionally softened to *u*. Whether the name therefore be read Nebu-kudar-russor or Nebu-sadusar, or be given any intermediate form, I consider immaterial, the Babylonians having been evidently unable to appreciate nice distinctions of articulation. I further remark on the subject of Babylon, in Dr. Hincks's paper than are to be found about Hillah and Baghdad. The ruins of Niffer are more extensive than those of Babylon, and the bricks are stamped with the name of an independent king, of which, as it is expressed entirely by monograms, I cannot ascertain the phonetic form[1]. At Warka, again, which was known to the Talmudists and early Arabs as the birth-place of Abraham, and which is even named Ur, in the early Arab geographers, thus showing positively that it is the Ur of the Chaldees, and the Orchoe of the Greeks,—at this place the ruins are of a stupendous character, and, judging from the fragments only which I have seen of the bricks, the name of the king is different from any yet known[2]. There are other ruins at Umgheir

(page 41) that he takes the word 𒀭 𒀭𒀭 for a special title, and draws an inference from the use of this word in the Khorsabad Inscriptions, that the monarch was actual king of Assyria, but only lord paramount of Babylon. If Dr. Hincks, however, will refer to the British Museum series, Pl. 12, l. 9, he will find the term 𒀭 𒀭𒀭 used as a simple conjunction to connect the names of the two gods ◄ and ►►𒌋, and will thus, I think, see sufficient reason for reading the title of the Khorsabad monarch as " king of Assyria and Babylonia."

[1] I have twice visited Niffer, which is in Lat. 32° 7' 3", and Long. 45° 15', and have minutely examined the ruins. The name of the king is 𒀭 𒀭 𒀭, and the countries over which he rules are called Sarrakam and Kabsikar, both of these names being also found on the Warka bricks, and the latter, slightly varied in the orthography, being repeated on a very remarkable stone in the British Museum, and being also mentioned in the East India-House Inscription, col. 7, l. 15. I consider Kabsikar or Kartsikar to be the Cascara of the Greeks, and كسكر of the Arabs, the name of the province in which Niffer was situated; while Sarrakam may possibly be the Soracte of Pliny, a most ancient city of Babylonia, which he ascribes to Semiramis. Niffer is mentioned by the early Arab traditionists as one of the four primæval cities of the world, and is also said to have been the original capital of Babylonia. It was the see of a Christian bishopric in comparatively modern times.

[2] The following extracts from a very ancient and valuable Manuscript in my library, called Tiráz-el-Mejális, will I think, determinately connect the ruins of Warka with the Biblical Ur of the Chaldees, as far at any rate as local tradition may be trusted. " The traditionists report that Abraham was born at El Warka (الورك), in the district of Edh-Dhawábi (الذوابى), on the confines of Kaskar, and that his father afterwards moved to Nimrud's capital, which was in the territory of Kutha. As-sudi, however, states, that when the mother of Abraham found herself pregnant, Azer (the Biblical Terah) feared lest

G

and Umwaweis, not less interesting, and all built of bricks stamped with inscriptions recording the royal founders. In this country, indeed, of Lower Chaldæa, we must look for Taha Dunis, Beth Takkara, Beth Eden, &c., which were flourishing and important cities at the earliest Assyrian period[1].

The neighbouring country of Susiana also is rich in ancient sites. It would be particularly interesting to excavate the great mound of Susa, for an obelisk which is still lying on the mound, and which bears a long inscription of king Susra[2], attests the existence of sculptured slabs, and there are also good grounds for supposing we might find bilingual legends, that is, hieroglyphic legends with Cuneiform translations, a monument of this class having certainly been preserved at Susa until within the last few years. The Cuneiform character, however, employed at Susa, is the farthest removed of any from the original Assyrian type, and as the language also appears to be quite different from Babylonian,—not even as I think of the Semitic family,— the decipherment of the inscriptions would require a distinct and very laborious study.

There is still one more class of inscriptions, in a variety of the Assyrian character, which I term Elymæan. They are found in

---

the child should perish; so he went out with her to a country between Kufa and Wasit, which was called Ur (اروٖ), and concealed her in a cave, where she was delivered." Strabo mentions the Chaldæans of Orchoe in conjunction with those of Borsippa, and the city is noticed by all the geographers. I have not met with any Cuneiform name that will suit the Greek or Arabic orthography, unless it be the city of ⸢cuneiform⸣, mentioned in the Inscription on Bellino's Cylinder, side 3, l. 28; and I cannot venture to draw any conclusion from a single notice. Mr. Loftus is at present employed in excavating the ruins of Warka, and will soon probably communicate to the world some account of his discoveries.

[1] It should be remembered that Arrian places the tombs of the ancient Assyrian kings in this particular quarter, and that in the Peutingerian tables the same monuments are laid down with a precision that can leave no doubt of their having once existed, in the marshes south of Babylon. The Arabs, also, have very remarkable notices regarding Atet, Ba-nikáya, Hakeh, Haffeh and other ancient sites in this vicinity, of which nothing is at present known.

[2] The Cuneiform orthography of the name is ⸢cuneiform⸣, and the father's name is perhaps Tarbadus ⸢cuneiform⸣, though it is not easy to distinguish some of the characters. It would be impossible, I may add, to publish this Inscription without casting a new type, the characters being fully as complicated as the forms employed in Babylonian and Assyrian Hieratic.

Elymais proper, and as in all probability they merely record the actions of provincial governors, or of kings tributary to Susa, the contents of them would hardly prove of any extraordinary interest. The character of these inscriptions is sensibly modified from the Assyrian and Babylonian type, and varies equally much from the character employed at the neighbouring city of Susa, yet it is not very difficult to be deciphered, and if the language were only approximately known, the general contents of the legends might be discovered. I can make nothing, however, of the language. It appears to me to be Scythic, rather than Semitic or Indo-European, but the materials are too scanty to afford grounds for any trustworthy analysis[1].

I have thus, I believe, cursorily noticed all the various classes of Cuneiform Inscriptions, connected with the Assyrian type. Undoubtedly, through the partial intelligence which we have as yet alone acquired of their contents, a most important avenue has been opened to our knowledge of the ancient world. Nations whom we have hitherto viewed exclusively through the dim medium of myth, or of tradition, now take their definite places in history; but before we can affiliate these nations on any sure ethnological grounds—before we can trace their progress to civilization or their relapse into barbarism —before we can estimate the social phases through which they have passed—before we can fix their chronology, identify their monarchs, or even individualize each king's career, much patient labour must be encountered—much ingenuity must be exercised—much care must be bestowed on collateral, as well as intrinsic evidence, and above all, instead of the fragmentary materials which are at present alone open to our research, we must have consecutive monumental data, extending at least, over the ten centuries which preceded the reign of Cyrus the Great.

---

[1] See British Museum series, Pls. 31, 32, and 36, 37. I perceive from a foot note in page 62 of Dr. Hincks's paper on the Khorsabad Inscriptions, that he has also observed the apparent similarity between the language of the Elymæan Inscriptions and that of the second column of the trilingual tablets, though he admits neither one nor the other to be of the Scythic family. I shall publish the Behistun translations in the so-called Median dialect with all convenient dispatch, and the question of lingual type can hardly remain after that a subject of much controversy. Whether at the same time the Elymæan language was really of the same family I am not prepared to say, without a more careful examination of the Inscriptions than I have yet been able to undertake.

LONDON:

PRINTED BY HARRISON AND SON,
ST. MARTIN'S LANE.